Mons. Chappe d´Auteroche

A voyage to California, to observe the transit of Venus

Mons. Chappe d´Auteroche

A voyage to California, to observe the transit of Venus

ISBN/EAN: 9783741180699

Manufactured in Europe, USA, Canada, Australia, Japa

Cover: Foto ©Andreas Hilbeck / pixelio.de

Manufactured and distributed by brebook publishing software (www.brebook.com)

Mons. Chappe d´Auteroche

A voyage to California, to observe the transit of Venus

A
VOYAGE
TO
CALIFORNIA,
TO OBSERVE THE
TRANSIT OF VENUS.

BY
Mons. CHAPPE D'AUTEROCHE.

WITH AN
HISTORICAL DESCRIPTION
OF THE
AUTHOR's ROUTE THROUGH MEXICO,
AND THE
NATURAL HISTORY OF THAT PROVINCE.

ALSO, A
VOYAGE
TO
NEWFOUNDLAND AND SALLEE,
TO MAKE EXPERIMENTS ON
MR. LE ROY's TIME KEEPERS.

BY
Monsieur DE CASSINI.

LONDON:
PRINTED FOR EDWARD AND CHARLES DILLY,
IN THE POULTRY.
MDCCLXXVIII.

ADVERTISEMENT.

THESE Voyages were undertaken on important occasions, and executed by Gentlemen eminent in their respective walks of Science, for the public utility. The performances were so well approved by the French nation, that they went through several editions, and the Translator hopes that they will be received with equal pleasure by every English reader.—Many of the remarks and observations contained in them, must be allowed to be very interesting to the Public, and the whole contents entertaining and instructive.

CONTENTS.

	Page
VOYAGE to Mexico	1
Astronomical experiments and observations	9
Arrival at Vera Cruz	15
Description of the harbour and town of Vera Cruz	16
Route through the Province of Mexico	27
Description of the City of Mexico	40
Passage from San Blas to California	55
Natural History of Mexico	77

Voyage to Newfoundland	109
Trial of a lock to ascertain what way a ship makes	112
Method of curing and salting the green cod	120

Description

CONTENTS.

	Page
Description of Saint Pierre	138
Manner of preparing and drying the cod	145
Cautions as to the road of St. Pierre	154
Observations on the Time Keepers at that place	158
Voyage from St. Pierre to Sallee	160
Description of Sallee	168
———— of the tower of Assan	179
Voyage to Cadiz	201
Account of Cadiz	205
Observations on the Time Keepers at that place	209
Voyage from Cadiz to Brest	212

VOYAGE

VOYAGE
TO
MEXICO
AND
CALIFORNIA.

I Set out from Paris September 18, 1768, for Havre de Grace, where I was to embark.' I was attended by a servant, and

' Mr. Chappe's Journal begins but at his departure from Cadiz to Vera Cruz. All the facts I relate in the beginning of this account, previous to that period, are collected from his own letters, and from the accounts of his fellow travellers.

B   by

by three other persons, who had engaged to go along with me to California, and to share the labours and dangers of so long a voyage. Mr. Pauly, the King's Engineer and Geographer, from whose talents I expected great assistance, was to second me in my astronomical and geographical operations: Mr. Noel, a pupil of the Academy of Painting, was intended for our draughtsman, to take draughts of sea coasts, plants, animals, and whatever we might meet with that was curious: lastly, Mr. Dubois, a watchmaker, was intrusted with the care of preserving my instruments, and repairing the little mischiefs they too often sustain in such long voyages.

Whoever considers the prodigious extent of a passage of several thousand leagues, such as I was going to undertake; and reflects that one unlucky moment, the least intervening cloud, might in one day defeat all our hopes, and render fruitless so much toil and expence, will not wonder at my taking thefe precautions, to draw other advantages from this voyage: that in cafe we fhould be fo unfortunate as to fail in our main purpofe, we might in fome meafure make amends to the learned world for this lofs. Aftronomy, geography, phyfic, and natural hiftory, were the objects I propofed. If the apparatus and materials requifite for that purpofe were both cumberfome and coftly, I was fully repaid by the pleafing hopes of improving my voyage to more purpofes than one.

I arrived at Havre de Grace on the 21ft of September, and found the fhip *Le Nouveau Mercure*, commanded by Captain Le Clerc, ready to fail for Cadiz. I embarked the 27th with my company and inftruments, and we fet fail the next day. We had a very rough paffage; a hard gale that we met with north of Cape Finifterre, left the fea very tempeftuous for near a week after. The winds were almoſt always contrary, ſo that we were one and twenty days going from Havre to Cadiz, which is commonly done in half the time.

We arrived at Cadiz October 17. The Spaniſh fleet which was to convey us to Vera Cruz, had already been in the road a whole month, and ſeemed ready to ſail. This gave me joy at firſt, little knowing how diſtant that departure was, which to me ſeemed ſo near; ſtill leſs did I foreſee the difficulties I was to encounter, joined with the tedioufneſs of a delay, which a thouſand times made me deſpair of getting in time to California.

The very moment I landed, I haſtened to wait on the governor of Cadiz, the intendant of the navy, and the Marquis de Tilly, general of the fleet. Theſe gentlemen received me with the greateſt civility.

lity. Mr. de Tilly having fignified to me the orders of his court, by which he was enjoined to take me on board his fleet, with only a watchmaker and a draughtfman, I was in the utmoft aftonifhment to find that no mention was made of Mr. Pauly, my fecond. I reprefented to M. de Tilly that this omiffion, falling juft upon the very man I could leaft fpare, muft be merely owing to a miftake: he was very fenfible it was fo, and affured me that on his part I fhould meet with no difficulty in the affair. But unfortunately, the embarking of the paffengers was not wholly in his power; it principally concerned the Marquis de Real Theforo, prefident of the *Contractation*, and to him we were to apply. Then it was that I met with frefh obftacles.

In the orders of the court, communicated by the intendant to the prefident of the contractation, no mention was made but

but of me. The latter confequently, far from allowing Mr. Pauly to attend me, would make out no order but for myfelf alone, and only one inftrument.

It is eafy to conceive what I fuffered from thefe unexpected difappointments. At firft fight, they appeared to me fuch as might eafily be removed by only explaining the matter, but I was foon convinced nothing was to be expected that way. I therefore difpatched a courier to the Marquis d'Offun, our ambaffador at Madrid, to acquaint him of my fituation, and defire him to procure from the court of Spain fuch precife orders, as fhould leave no room for any more cavilling. The courier returned in about a week, and all was at length fettled to my fatisfaction. I therefore fent my inftruments on board the commodore, and impatiently waited for the moment when I could myfelf embark with all my attendants.

I had

I had already lingered a whole month at Cadiz, and the time of our departure was ſtill uncertain. When I calculated the time it would take to reach Vera Cruz, then to travel three hundred leagues by land to San-Blas, and afterwards to croſs the Vermeille ſea to California, I foreſaw it was morally impoſſible we ſhould get there in time for our obſervation, if we were retarded ever ſo little longer. I wrote to the Marquis d'Oſſun, requeſting, that in caſe the fleet did not ſail immediately, I might be permitted to embark on board the firſt ſhip, no matter which, provided we might be conveyed to Vera Cruz without loſs of time, and ſail as ſwift as poſſible.

The court of Spain, ſenſible of the neceſſity of taking ſuch a ſtep, readily acquieſced, as our requeſt could only be dictated by a zeal for the undertaking. Orders were iſſued, in caſe the fleet ſhould be be delayed, inſtantly to fit out a Bilander, or light veſſel to tranſport me to Vera Cruz, together with Meſſieurs Doz and Medina, two navy officers, and aſtronomers to his Catholic Majeſty, deſtined to obſerve the tranſit of Venus jointly with me, and at the ſame place.

This freſh order from court ſoon changed the face of affairs. At laſt I ſaw the wiſhed-for moment that had ſo long deluded my hopes. A veſſel with only twelve hands, was fitted out in a trice. I was ſtill more expeditious in removing my inſtruments that were on board the Commodore ſhip. The frailty of the veſſel I was going to venture in, and on which account ſome people endeavoured to intimidate me, was in my eyes but one merit the more. Judging of her ſwiftneſs by her lightneſs, I preferred her to the fineſt ſhip of the line. At length we ſet ſail, and at that inſtant I felt a tranſport of of joy, which was not to be equalled till I landed in California.

I shall not trouble the reader with the journal of our paſſage from Cadiz to Vera Cruz*, as it offers nothing but what is common to all long voyages. Every kind of weather, calms, ſtorms, winds, sometimes fair, ſometimes contrary; ſuch is in few words the hiſtory of moſt voyages; and as to ours, we may add, a continual toſſing of our little nut-ſhell, which was ſo very light as to be the ſport of the ſmalleſt wave.

I ſpent the whole time of our voyage in making phyſical and aſtronomical experiments and obſervations; ſuch as, comparing the height of the different

---

* Here begins Mr. Chappe's regular journal. I thought it beſt to ſuppreſs the particulars of a tedious navigation, as it muſt be tireſome to the reader, and contains nothing that is curious.

thermometers, some plunged into the sea at different depths, others in open air; I ascertained the declination and inclination of the magnetic needle in different latitudes; lastly, I made several observations relative to the distance of the moon from the stars. I will not conceal the difficulties I met with when I endeavoured to make use of the *megameter* for these observations.[a] I tried several times to use this instrument, and never could succeed but once, when the ship was quite steady; that time, I got the moon full in the lens, which I never could when the sea was in motion. Per-

[a] It is proper to take notice, that the following reflections on the several instruments for taking obfervations at sea, and ascertaining longitudes, are taken almost word for word from Mr. Chappe's own journal; I have never allowed myself to add any thing in matters which might be of some moment, especially where the author has notions peculiar to himself.

haps

haps this was for want of practice; however, I was obliged to have recourse to the octant, which I employed with much more ease and success. I attempted in vain to observe Jupiter's satellites with the new telescope proposed to the academy by Abbé Rochon. Indeed the field of this telescope was rather too small; I saw Jupiter plain enough, but could not see the satellites.

All these trials suggested to me that it will be a hard matter to succeed in inventing instruments of easy use at sea, if they rest upon nothing more than the hand of the observer. One remark more I shall make on the determination of longitudes by distances of the moon from the stars. The tedious calculations which this method requires, with the accuracy and attention requisite in the observation itself, make it doubtful to me whether it will ever be fit for the use of trading vessels.

It

It must be confessed, it requires no small degree of resolution, even in persons best acquainted with these studies, to add to the fatigues of the sea, those of a nice observation, and of the tedious calculations consequent upon it. This convinces me that the use of time-keepers, from its extreme ease, will be found to be of more general service in the navy; it requires no instruments but what seamen are accustomed to; no nicety is wanted in the observation; lastly, the calculation is short and easy; a most important advantage this, in many cases, and particularly at sea.

These several operations, to which I devoted the whole time of our passage, made it appear less tedious, and helped me to pass away with some pleasure the seventy-seven days it lasted. I must say that the sea-faring life is tiresome and uniform to such only as have not accustomed

cuftomed themfelves to look about them, and who behold all nature with an eye of indifference; but to an attentive fpectator, the fea offers objects very capable of entertaining the mind, and exercifing all the intellectual powers. Nature has beauties even in her horrors; nay, it is there perhaps that fhe is moft admirable and fublime. The calmnefs of a fine day is in fome meafure lefs interefting than thofe moments of diftrefs, when the waves, lifted up by the winds, feem confounded with the fky. Deep gulphs are opening every moment. At this inftant, man fhudders at the fight of a danger that appears inevitable; but anon, when he fees the calm fucceed the tempeft, his admiration turns upon himfelf, upon the veffel, upon the pilot, who are come off conquerors over the moft formidable elements. A fecret pride then rifes in his mind; he fays within himfelf
" If man, as an individual, is but a fpeck,
" an atom in this vaft univerfe, he is, by
" his

" his genius and his daring spirit, worthy
" to embrace its whole extent, and to
" penetrate into the wonders it contains."

Nothing indeed gives a higher notion of the compass of the human mind, than that art, now brought to such perfection, of steering safely over the trackless ocean, and on a floating mansion, to traverse immense spaces, in spite of two combined elements. Who that reflects on the numberless dangers of the sea, but must cry out with Horace :

> Illi robur & æs triplex
> Circa pectus erat, qui fragilem truci
> Commisit pelago ratem.

This is what I repeated a thousand times on our voyage, thinking on Christopher Colomb, Gryalva, and all those first intrepid mariners, who, in quest of a new world, upon a mere surmise of its existence, suggested by their own genius, dared

dared to undertake near, three hundred years ago, those very voyages which at this day we still account dangerous, though assisted with a thousand helps that were wanting in the days of those great men.

We arrived at Vera Cruz on the 6th of March, 1769, about two in the afternoon. We cast anchor within a league and half of the coast, intending next morning to double the breakers that defend the entrance of the harbour, but could not reach them till the 8th, when we entered the canal. Then it was, that finding ourselves surrounded on all sides by threatening rocks, we made a signal for a pilot, and hoisted French colours, but this was the ready way to get no assistance. Mr. Doz and Mr. Medina had wisely advised our captain to hoist Spanish colours, but he would not, and from this we had well nigh perished.

It

It seems the entrance into the port of Vera Cruz being prohibited to all foreign ships, our signal had been answered by the firing of a gun, to compel us to anchor in the canal; this was devoting us to certain destruction. The canal leads to the harbour among rocks which stand so close, that there is but just room for one ship to get through. The wind then blew from the north, and bearing full upon the rocks, made it exceedingly dangerous to anchor in such a narrow pass. Yet we were forced to comply, from an express order sent us by a sloop.

So critical was our position, that of a hundred vessels which anchor there, not two escaped, as we were told afterwards. There we remained, in the cruel expectation of seeing ourselves every moment dashed against the surrounding rocks, till the Governor of Vera Cruz being informed that our ship though a French bottom,

came

came thither by order of the court of Spain, sent us leave to come in. This message was as joyfully received as it had been impatiently expected. We weighed anchor, and at last entered the harbour of Vera Cruz, after a passage of seventy-seven days, having sailed from Cadiz the 21st of December. It was high time our voyage should be at an end, for our whole provision was reduced to one sheep, five fowls, and water for a week at most. The hurry with which our vessel was equipped at Cadiz, did not allow us to take all the necessary precautions for so long a voyage. Half our live provisions died within the first fortnight, and great part of the others had been thrown overboard. In other respects, we had a tolerable passage, till these last moments; which indeed were cruel ones, as we saw ourselves ready to perish at the very mouth of the harbour, thanks to our flag that

C   ought

ought to have protected us, considering the alliance between both nations.

Mr. Doz and Mr. Medina went ashore first, to confer with the governor, who sent me a boat two hours after. I stepped in with Mr. Pauly my second. That north wind, which we had so long dreaded in the canal, increased hourly, and already blew so vehemently as to make our landing difficult; however, we got safe ashore, but another boat that came after us, had four of her men blown overboard, who with much ado saved their lives by swimming ashore.

I had no sooner entered the town, but it blew a most furious hurricane. All intercourse with our ship was then cut off. She had barely time to run for shelter behind the castle of St. Juan d'Ulua, the only place where a ship can be screened from the north wind. For three days

days that this storm lasted, I was in the greatest anxiety for my instruments, and for my people whom I had left behind, as it was impossible to land them, and I well knew their safety depended entirely upon the strength of the cables with which they were moored. Had these cables broken or given way, they must inevitably have perished before our eyes, without a possibility of giving them the least assistance. Every year affords but too many instances of the like disasters, which make the port of Vera Cruz very formidable. We were so lucky as not to add to the dreadful list. The calm returned, and I eagerly seized the first moments to land all my effects and my attendants; then it was that I felt the transporting pleasure of being all once more together in a place of safety, and delivered from those anxieties which are unavoidable upon so inconstant an element as the sea. The passage that ſtill lay before us to California, was to be more fatiguing but leſs dangerous.

The governor of Vera Cruz was juſt dead, and the deputy Governor acted in his ſtead, till the Viceroy ſhould appoint another: he it was who received us, and he loaded us with civilities the whole time we ſtaid there. This was not long; only as much as was neceſſary to prepare for our next voyage. The place offers nothing that was worth ſtaying for.

La Vera Cruz is ſituated by the ſea ſide, in the ſouthern part of Mexico. It is ſurrounded on the north with barren ſands, and on the weſt with bogs that have been drained; this makes the ſituation both diſagreeable and unwholeſome. What I have already ſaid, ſufficiently ſhews how dangerous a harbour it is; the guſts of north wind, ſo frequent in the gulph of Mexico, are much to be dreaded here.

here. Nevertheless, this port is much frequented, especially once in two years, when the Spanish fleet comes thither, to unload the European goods, which are afterwards to be sold, and distributed all over Mexico, and to bring home that silver and those immense treasures, the thirst of which, cost the lives of so many thousands, and made the wretched subjects of Montezuma the sad victims of the insatiable greediness of the Europeans.

La Vera Cruz contains no grand edifice. The Governor's house has nothing that distinguishes it from the rest, which are all built after the Spanish manner. There is one church and three monasteries. The streets are tolerably strait, and of a common breadth. The town is encompassed with walls, and has four gates, each flanked with two towers. There are two bastions at the ends of the wall next the water side. These fortifications are in a

sad

sad condition; the best defence is the fortress belonging to the castle of S. Juan d'Ulua. It is built on a rock which rises in the middle of the harbour, facing the town at some distance. A deputy lodges and commands in this castle, and is independent of the governor of Vera Cruz, who commands in the town.

The day we landed, the governor's substitute wrote to the viceroy to inform him of our arrival: the latter soon sent orders to facilitate our further voyage, and that we should be furnished with as many men and mules as we wanted, to carry our baggage and instruments.

From Vera Cruz to St. Blas (where we were to embark, in order to cross the Vermeille sea) we had to travel about three hundred leagues, partly through desart lands, and by the worst roads imaginable. It is easily conceived, what
trouble

trouble we had in preparing for such a long and inconvenient journey. First, we were obliged to unpack all our things and to make them up in small loads, fit for mules to carry; consequently, we wanted a great many beasts; the more as we were under a necessity of carrying our beds and tents along with us, being to halt in places destitute of habitations. Next came the care of providing food: We were told we should find few resources that way along the road. The Indians feed upon poor bread, made of the meal of Indian corn; they grind it the best they can between two stones, and tempering the coarse flour with a little water, they make it into cakes, which they bake upon a flat stone, clapping it on the middle of a great fire. These loaves, which they call *tortillas*, are not much better than sea-biscuit, of which we had made a small provision.

As to the other meſſes that the Indians feaſt upon, they put in ſo much pimento, and pour ſuch bad oil over them, that it is impoſſible, eſpecially for a Frenchman, to touch a bit. We therefore bought at Vera Cruz a great quantity of hams, and ſalt *pampano*. I muſt not omit ſpeaking of this fiſh.

The *pampano* is very plenty in the ſouthern part of the gulph of Mexico; it is caught from February to April; after that, there is no more to be found. This fiſh is commonly a foot and a half long, and about ſix inches wide; it has no ſcales; the ſkin, which is perfectly ſmooth, is of a ſlate colour, inclining to a pearly white, and grows yellowiſh towards the belly. The *pampano* has no teeth; the fleſh is exceedingly nice: the Spaniards extol it above all other ſea fiſh. Indeed we found it excellent good, freſh; but when ſalted it is very indifferent. We took

took some to eat upon the road, only for want of something better; and could not even preserve it long, the weather being very hot.

Two other kinds of fish abound in the rivers about Vera Cruz; the one is called *sargo*, in Spanish, and appears to me to be the same as our turbot; the other is called *corobo*, which in Spanish signifies *hump backed*, and is expressive of its shape. As these fish are very common, it is needless to describe them.

The quadrupeds found at Vera Cruz and in Mexico are the same as in Europe: but among the insects, there is one that deserves particular notice, and this is the *nigua*.

The *nigua* is black, somewhat like a flea, and as small. It commonly fastens to the feet or hands, and by degrees works itself

itself into the flash, which it gnaws, and at last causes violent itchings. It wraps itself up in a bag of the size of a pea, and there lays its eggs. If it is left too long in the wound, or if in picking it out you happen to burst it, the part is found full of the animal's eggs, and you are forced to cut away all the flesh that is infected with this vermin. But the worst is, that the wound, they tell you, proves mortal if any water is suffered to touch it. And indeed, the first thing persons do, after they have extracted the *nigua*, is to fill up the hole with tallow. This insect is very common about Vera Cruz; the Indians have their feet sadly mauled by them, and all distorted by the incisions they are forced to make whenever they are stung. It appears that this insect is likewise found in a province of Peru. Frezier*, in his account of a voyage to the

* Account of a south sea voyage to the coasts of Chili and Peru, p. 214.

south sea, gives nearly the same particulars, but calls the insect *pico*. I should think this must be less venomous than the *nigua* of Vera Cruz, for he says nothing of the deadly effect of water.

We left Vera Cruz the 18th of March in the evening, and took the road to Mexico. We had hired two litters, one for Mr. Doz and Mr. Medina, the other for Mr. Pauly and myself; the rest rode on mules, and went before, with the Indians who drove our baggage. We kept along the sea shore for two hours, advancing to the north west, and then turned off to the inland country through immense woods. In three hours we came to a river, on the other side of which is a village called *Vieja Vera Cruz*. This is the spot where Vera Cruz formerly stood. The river that runs at the foot of this old Vera Cruz is about as broad as the Seine; you cross it in a large ferry-boat,

boat, railed in on both sides with beams about ten foot high. We saw nothing remarkable in this forsaken town, which is now but a very small village, inhabited by none but Indians; but what made this place very comfortable for us, was, the good refreshments we found there, and particularly wheaten bread, far better than what we had enjoyed at New Vera Cruz. We were told we should meet with no more such all the rest of the way, so we laid in of it for four or five days. This was such luck as travellers must make much of.

The following day we set out for *Xalapa,* the next town, and distant from Vieja Vera Cruz about two days journey. We found upon the road only a few little hamlets, consisting of two or three houses each, sometimes but one, and in these a traveller can hardly get water to quench his thirst. From Vieja Vera Cruz to the hermitage

hermitage of *las Animas*, which is about fifteen leagues, not one spring or brook is to be met with, to quench that intolerable thirst occasioned by the vehement heat, and the dust raised by the mules. Sometimes indeed, you meet with Indian women, stationed on the road, who sell milk to travellers. They commonly keep at some distance from the road, and even hide behind a tree or bush; so that you must be acquainted with their tricks, or you would be never the better for them. They will let travellers go by, especially if they be foreigners, without ever offering them any of their milk; but our Indian guides gave us notice whenever they spied any of these women: we made up to them, and they conducted us to a little hut made of shrubs, where we found a cow, and there we quenched our thirst at a very small expence. We did not meet with this good luck so often as we wished.

In the fine countries of Europe, where conveniencies of every kind abound upon the high roads, the traveller perceives a change of climate only by a change of enjoyments; but with us it was far otherwise. Excessive heat, frightful roads, and the flowness of our mules of burden, hardly suffered us to travel at the rate of ten leagues a day, which made our journey very tedious and tiresome. Nothing interesting to make us amends. We traversed on uncultivated lands or forests, and saw nothing but rude nature. I confess she is not without her beauties; but in time the eye grows weary of them; uniformity grows insipid, variety only has charms, and this the traveller seeks when he goes from country to country.

We arrived at Xalapa the 21st of March. This town, which stands close to a mountain, is divided into two parts; the one is at the foot, the other on the flope of the mountain. The houses are of stone, and pretty well built, but there is no remarkable edifice. A confiderable trade is carried on at Xalapa, which, every two years brings thither a great many Spaniards and Indians, who come towards the month of March. Then it is, that for the fpace of fix weeks, a famous fair is held, where all the merchandizes brought to Vera Cruz by the Spanifh fleet, and from thence by land to Xalapa are fold, and afterwards retailed all over Mexico. Thefe European commodities confift of cloth, filks, muflins, linen of all forts, but chiefly fine clear lawns from Britany, toys, fteel, iron work, &c. The Mexicans give in exchange cochineal and money, for as to gold or filver bullion, no body is allowed to have any, and the exportation of it is ftrictly prohibited. A breach of the regulations refpecting the mines, is the greateft crime that can be committed

committed in Mexico. A falfe coiner is hanged, a murderer is only imprifoned or banifhed.

I had feveral letters of recommendation, which had been given me at Cadiz for fome merchants fettled at Xalapa, but as we came in very late, and were defirous of fetting out early the next morning, I put off delivering them till my return. The environs of Xalapa exhibited what we had feldom feen fince we left Vera Cruz, cultivated grounds, trees of all forts, thick groves, a'l which befpoke a fertile foil; and indeed very good Indian corn grows about Xalapa.

Juft without the town we found a handfome caufeway, walled in on both fides, which led to the top of the mountain. It is a hard road, and would be a very pleafant one if not fo fleep; indeed the mountain is
extremely

extremely high. When we got to the top, we enjoyed a moſt ſingular proſpect; for we ſtood ſo high that the clouds were our horizon. At ſome diſtance from Xalapa, I begun to obſerve iron lying in blackiſh ſtrata along the road. Soon after, the ſoil ſhewed evident tokens of an extinguiſhed volcano. In ſome places, a light moſs hardly covered dry ſtones and lavas that lay acroſs the road; which ſeemed to me to indicate that this volcano, wherever it was, had not been long extinguiſhed, as theſe lavas were not yet covered with earth. Nature, in this place, bore the marks of the greateſt diſorder.

From Xalapa to *Las-Bigas*, the next hamlet, diſtant about ſix leagues, we did nothing but go up and down hill, croſſing a ridge of mountains that extends in breadth to both theſe places. The hamlet of *Las-Bigas*, like thoſe we had met with before we got to Xalapa, conſiſts
D   only

only of two or three houses, but they are better built. From Vera Cruz, the Indian huts are made with reeds, placed perpendicularly, and even at some distance apart, so that they are but poorly sheltered from the weather; besides, all along the house, between the roof and the top of the wall that supports it, they leave a space or opening for an outlet to the smoke, their fire being made in the middle of the room. But beyond Xalapa, as the ground is higher and higher, and consequently the temperature of the air colder, the dwellings are much tighter and closer. The walls are of stone, and in many places of stone calcined in some volcano. These calcined stones are very common in those regions.

The inhabitants of Las-Bigas are mulattoes; the women go half naked, and shew a most frightful neck. The usual dress of the Indian women consists of two pieces

pieces of stuff, one that is fixed about their waist, and hangs half way down their legs in the shape of a petticoat; and the other, like a tablecloth, wraps over their shoulders, and covers them down to the waist. This kind of a cloak, which they call *pagnorobos*, they seldom wear but when they go abroad; at home they commonly pull it off, and so remain half naked. As to the men, they wear linen trousers, much like those of the sailors, and over these another pair made with skin. Their body is covered with a waistcoat without sleeves, or else they throw a woollen thing over their shoulders, like the women's pagnorobos. In some places far remote from any town, they go almost totally naked.

The Indians are of an olive complexion, have black eyes and hair, stout legs, and a flat nose. The women are of the same colour, and no very pleasing figures: they
commonly

commonly marry at nine or ten years old, and bear children till they are thirty-five or forty, but they seldom can rear a large family. The small pox and measles carry off a great many children, especially when the Indians, in order to cure them, put them into a sweating bath, which almost instantly kills them.

The ill treatment these poor Indians receive from their masters, contributes as much as sickness to destroy the race; and the mines where they make them work, yearly prove fatal to an infinite number of these poor wretches. The immense labours they have gone through at Mexico in draining the lake, have likewise been the death of many thousands; insomuch that the province of Mexico is now but a vast desert, compared to what it was in the time of Montezuma.

The

PROVINCE of MEXICO.

The Governor of Vera Cruz had written to the Viceroy of Mexico before we left the place, to inform him of the route we intended to take. The Viceroy, in confequence of this information, had done us the favour to fend us equipages from Mexico. We met them at *Perotte*, a hamlet, about forty leagues from the capital.

We were four days going from Perotte to Mexico. The road, which is pleafant, and moftly fmooth, is carried on between two ridges of mountains, which in fome places come pretty clofe together, and in others leave room for very extenfive plains. A little beyond Perotte, we began to fee the famous mountain of *Orifaba*, faid to be the higheft in Mexico. When we got to the hamlet of *Sant-Yago*, we were but two leagues from this mountain, which then exhibited a moft pleafing profpect.

Its top was wholly covered with snow, whilst the foot displayed the lovely verdure of rich cultivated land. This mountain of Orisaba is seen from Mexico, which is no less than twenty leagues distant.

Along this road from Perotte to the capital, you find large quantities of calcined stones scattered about in many places. The village of *Hapa* especially is surrounded with it, and all the houses are built with this stone. We arrived at this village on Good Friday evening. This day of sad solemnity for the Roman church, is not less so to the Mexicans than to us, but they have an odd way of keeping it. As we entered the village we met a very numerous procession; at the head went a statue of the holy Virgin, carried by young women in masks: a great croud of people followed, likewise masked;
some

PROVINCE of MEXICO. 39

some with guitars, some with baſſoons, who played the moſt groteſque muſic; inſomuch that we ſhould rather have taken this proceſſion for a carnival maſquerade than a religious ceremony, had it not been for the prieſts who attended it, and whoſe gravity made the moſt ridiculous contraſt. Is this to be wondered at? Force of arms could make but very bad chriſtians of theſe people, and their ſtupidity has made them improve upon the ignorance and ſuperſtitious abuſes laid to the charge of the Spaniſh monks, who are moſtly entruſted with the care of the Indian-pariſhes.

We arrived at *Mexico* on Eaſter Day, March 26, at noon. Before we entered the city, we met the Marquis de la Torre, Inſpector of infantry. The moment he ſaw us, he went and gave notice of our arrival to the Viceroy, who ſent orders that
we

we should be suffered to enter the city without any search, and conducted to the house of the Jesuits, where a lodging was prepared for us. We had no sooner alighted there, but four gentlemen came to conduct us to the palace. I am at a loss for words to express the friendship and politeness shewn us by the Marquis de Croix, Viceroy of Mexico, and by his whole court. He left nothing undone to procure us whatever we wished for, and to make our stay at Mexico agreeable to us. We had no table but his own for the four days we continued in the town, and he was so obliging as to send a cook to dress victuals for our attendants after the French fashion. The next day after our arrival, he lent us one of his coaches to go about the town.

Mexico, the capital of the province which bears that name, is situated on the banks

banks of a lake, and built upon a fen, crossed by a multitude of canals, consequently the houses are all built upon piles. The ground gives way in many places, and many buildings are observed to have funk upwards of fix feet, without any visible alteration in the body of the building: one of these is the cathedral, which I shall speak of hereafter.

The streets of Mexico are very wide, perfectly strait, and almost all intersect each other at right angles. The houses are tolerably built, but not much ornamented either within or without; their make is the same as in Spain.

There is no very remarkable edifice at Mexico. The Viceroy's palace is in a spacious and pretty regular square, with a fountain in the middle. The only merit of this palace is, that it is built very solid. No decorations are to be found there.

Within

Within its circumference are three handsome court-yards, with each a fountain in the middle. The mint stands behind this palace, and is a noble building. Upwards of a hundred workmen are constantly employed there in coining piastres for the King of Spain, out of the enormous masses of silver brought thither by the owners of the mines, who exchange them for coin. It is said, about fourteen millions of piastres are struck yearly in this mint.

The most sumptuous buildings are the churches, chapels, and convents. There are a great many in this city, which are very richly ornamented, and among others the cathedral. The rail round the high altar is solid silver; and what is still more costly, there is a silver lamp, so capacious that three men get in to clean it: this lamp is enriched with figures of lions' heads, and other ornaments of pure gold.

The

The infide pillars are hung with rich crimfon velvet, enriched with a broad gold fringe. This profusion of riches in the churches at Mexico is not very furprising to whoever has feen the cathedral of Cadiz, and the immenfe treafures contained in it. Gold and precious ftones are there lavifhed upon the facred veffels and ornaments; and the images of the holy Virgin and other faints are either folid filver, or clad in the richeft garments.

The outfide of the cathedral of Mexico is unfinifhed, and likely to continue fo; they are afraid of increafing the weight of the building, which already begins to fink, as before noticed. I fhall fay nothing of the other churches; I believe there are as many as there are faints in the calendar.

The city of Mexico contains three fquares; the firft is the *Maior* or great fquare,

square fronting the palace, the cathedral, and the market-place, which is a double square surrounded with buildings: This square is in the center of the city. The second, adjoining to this, is the square called *del Volador*, where the bull-feasts are held. The third, is that of *Santo Domingo*. These squares are tolerably regular, and each has a fountain in the middle. To the north of the town, near the suburbs, is the public walk, or *Alámeda*. A rivulet runs all round it, and forms a pretty large square, with a bason and *jet d'eau* in the middle. Eight walks, with each two rows of trees, terminate at this bason like a star; but as the soil of Mexico is unfit for trees, they are not in a very thriving condition. This is the only walk in or near to Mexico; all the country about it is swampy ground, and full of canals. A few paces off, and facing the Alameda, is the *Quemadero*: this is the place where they burn the Jews,

Jews, and other unhappy victims of the awful tribunal of Inquisition. This Quemadero is an enclosure between four walls, and filled with ovens, into which are thrown, over the walls, the poor wretches who are condemned to be burnt alive; condemned, by judges professing a religion whose first precept is Charity.

The short stay we made at Mexico did not permit me to take a fuller survey of the place. I was told there was a Spanish play-house, but I was not tempted to go. I had enough of one at Cadiz.

I found a Frenchman at Mexico who spoke the Spanish and Mexican languages tolerably well, and was perfectly acquainted with all this country, having lived in it many years. I took him for my interpreter, as I thought he would be very serviceable to me for the remainder of our journey, and especially in California.

As

As we went further on, we were to meet with Indians more savage than before; the Viceroy therefore thought proper to give us a guard of three soldiers, to defend us against the robbers who infest those parts. Troops of fierce and unconquered Indians, called by the Spaniards *Indios bravos*, attack travellers when they find themselves strongest, murder them, or at least, after stripping and tying them to the neighbouring trees, they carry off their mules and baggage to some bye places, known to none but themselves, where they share the money, and hide the rest of the booty. Our guides told us, that some of the forests and mountains we passed by, conceal immense treasures hoarded up by these banditti: they are easily known by a handkerchief which they hold between their teeth to hide their faces. When a traveller sees an Indian thus masked, the safest way is to be beforehand with him, and to kill him

if

if poſſible. We were ſo lucky as to meet with none. Having provided ourſelves with neceſſaries for our journey, we ſet out from Mexico the 30th of March, 1769. Mr. Doz and Mr. Medina had hired a wheel carriage, but for my part, as I had been told we ſhould meet with bad roads, I choſe to go on horſe-back. 'Tis true I did not ride the eaſier for it, but I eſcaped a thouſand miſchances which befell our two Spaniſh officers, and which retarded us more than once.

From Mexico to San-Blas, where we were to embark to croſs the Vermeillo ſea, they reckon about one hundred and ninety leagues. The farther you go from Mexico, the fewer habitations you meet with, and the road is often very rough, dangerous, and full of precipices. In moſt places where we ſtopped, we hardly found bread, and every thing in that part of the country wears the face of the moſt pinching penury.

Forty leagues from Mexico we found the little town of *Queretaro*, remarkable for a very famous manufactory of cloth. This town is pretty well built; it stands against the slope of a mountain, which is joined to another, farther off and higher, by a noble aqueduct, which conveys the water from the upper to the lower one, from whence it flows to all parts of the town. This aqueduct is a very solid piece of workmanship. These kind of works are very common in Mexico, and are the only remarkable performances in the way of building.

It was near Queretaro that I had the satisfaction, repeatedly to see a phænomenon realized, which I had oftener suspected than seen in France; I mean the lightning rising from the earth instead of issuing from the cloud, as it is commonly thought to do.

On the 3d of April in the evening, being then near *Molino*, a little hamlet about thirty-six leagues from Mexico, I observed to the south a great black cloud, at a moderate height above the horizon: the whole hemisphere about us had a fiery aspect. This cloud was supported, as it were, with three columns at equal distances, and their basis almost met the horizon. All the while it remained in this state, frequent and smart flashes of lightning appeared in three places of the cloud over these columns; and at the same time streams of electrical light darted from the correspondent points of the horizon below, as in an aurora borealis. Soon after, the cloud came lower down, and then it was that we saw incessant lightnings rising like so many sky rockets, and flashing at the top of the cloud. I was the more convinced that I was not mistaken, as in this observation, the first who took notice of the phænomenon were, all my attendants, the interpreter, the soldiers, none of whom could be under the influence of any syſtematic prejudice. Once only the lightning ſeemed to iſſue from the cloud. Two days after, we ſaw the ſame thing again, and plainly diſtinguiſhed the lightning riſing from the ground, nor was its motion ſo ſwift but what we could diſcern its origin and direction. The reader may ſee what I have ſaid on this ſubject in the Memoirs of the Academy for the year 1764, and in my Journey to Siberia.

Eight days after we had left Mexico, we arrived at *Guadalaxara*. This is a conſiderable town, and a biſhoprick. We reſted two days in this place; it was what I greatly wanted, after a journey of a hundred leagues, upon ſorry mules, and in bad weather and deteſtable roads.

The

The ninth we went from Guadalaxara, and lay at a fugar houfe called *Mutchitilté*. This place is furrounded with mountains, piled up, as it were, one above another, which make it a moft frightful fituation. From the middle of a rock, on the loftieft of thefe mountains, a fpring gufhes out, which falling two hundred feet perpendicular upon another rock below, forms a cafcade or fheet of water, which ftrikes the beholders with terror and admiration. It is impoffible to conceive a more frightful and dangerous road than that which we travelled for near five leagues after we left Mutchitilté; this road, which is hardly four feet wide, is cut on the flope of a mountain that rifes almoft perpendicular; the road is about half way up, fo that on one fide you are hemmed in by the mountain, and on the other in danger of falling down fuch deep precipices, that in fome places you hardly difcern the tops of the talleft tallest fir-trees in the vale below. To mend the matter, in this narrow pass we unluckily met a caravan of mules going the contrary way. What to do we did not know, and were much afraid for our mules that carried our larger instruments; however, we got clear of them, and soon came to a pretty good road, which brought us to the little town of *Tepik*, where we only stopt to eat our dinner, and hastened to San-Blas, where we arrived the next day, April 15, after spending twenty-eight days in crossing Mexico.

San-Blas is a very small hamlet, situate on the western coast of Mexico, at the mouth of the river *S. Pedro*. It is but within these few years that the Spaniards have made a settlement there, for the conveniency of transporting the troops and provisions they send into California.

The

The marquis de Croix, viceroy of Mexico, had long before sent orders to the commandant of San-Blas to hold a veſſel in readineſs to carry us over to California immediately upon our arrival. None of the paſſage boats happened to be in the harbour when he received this order, ſo that he had a little packet boat built on purpoſe with all expedition, and it was expected to be caulked and launched within ten days after our arrival; but we could not afford to wait ſo long. The paſſage from San-Blas to Cape San-Lucas is indeed but about ſixty leagues, but it ſometimes proves a very tedious and difficult one, owing to the calms and currents ſo frequent on the Vermeille ſea. We had no time to ſpare, as we were to make our obſervation the 3d of June. Very luckily for us, a packet boat came into the harbour the very evening of our arrival, which was immediately allotted for our ſervice. We fixed upon the fourth

fourth day for our departure, allowing ourselves but juſt time to provide victuals, and whatever elſe we were likely to want, in a country where nothing is to be got. The Spaniſh officers ſhipped materials on board the veſſel for erecting a complete obſervatory; for my part, I only took wherewithal to make a tent, and a great beam of cedar on which to hang up my clock.

The pilot gave us but poor encouragement, by telling us how, the year before, he had been one and twenty days going over from San-Blas to San-Lucas, and that, at a better ſeaſon of the year. This ſtartled me, and I was in ſome doubt whether it would not be more adviſeable to remain on the continent of Mexico, than to run the venture of being out at ſea at the time of the obſervation; but I ſoon found I muſt give up this ſcheme, on being told that the ſtated rains were going

VOYAGE to CALIFORNIA.

going to set in, before the end of May, and would continue with little or no interruption till the end of June. The best thing we could do was to put to sea, and endeavour to reach the opposite shore of the Vermeille sea, where we might hope for a clearer sky.

We sailed out of the harbour on the 19th of April, and soon found what the pilot had foretold. The first fortnight we were tantalized with calms, contrary winds and currents. At last, the 4th of May, for the first time, we steered full north, bearing for the cape; but there was so little wind, and that little was so often interrupted with calms, that we were near five days getting up to the port of Mazatan, about thirty-five leagues north of San-Blas. If we had gained a little in latitude, we had made very little progress in longitude. We then began to despair of getting to California in time for the obfervation, which would have been a moft cruel difappointment.

Our pilot thought he could perfectly account for the contrariety of the winds, by imputing it to the wrath of Heaven for our fins. This he endeavoured to avert by an offering to S. Francis Xaverius, which he laid upon the binacle, befeeching him to fend us a fair wind. The devout pilot's remedy did not prefently take effect, for the following days we had a fucceffion of calms and contrary winds.

Then indeed our fituation became every day more deplorable: our provifions begun to run fhort, efpecially the water: we were obliged to ftint ourfelves to a pint a day, and even this was deteftable water, having been put into vinegar cafks. All thefe trifles would have been nothing, could we have flattered ourfelves with fome gleam of hope. We were in the

25th

25th day of our paſſage, and only eighteen remained to the tranſit, and we were yet a great way from the place of our deſtination. It is true, that having gone pretty far north, the currents and the prevailing winds were now rather in our favour. From this time, it was my fixt reſolution to land at the firſt place we could reach in California; I little cared whether it was inhabited or deſart, ſo as I could but make my obſervation.

At laſt, by the help of ſome favourable gales and currents, we got ſight of the land of California, which we judged to be near Cape S. Lucar, diſtant about eighteen leagues: we drew near the next day with a gentle wind. The 18th at night we were but five leagues from land. I was ſtrenuous for landing at the neareſt place, but as I was ſingular in my opinion, the whole day was ſpent in altercations. The Spaniards wanted to go and land in

the

the bay of San-Barnabé, which was fifteen leagues farther, consequently this would have prolonged our navigation perhaps for several days; for in order to get at this bay, we had to encounter the north and north-west winds, which blew almost constantly. These gentlemen objected to me that we ventured the loss of the ship in landing at Cape San-Lucas; I made answer that I was confident his Catholic Majesty had rather lose a poor little pitiful vessel, than the fruits of so important an expedition as ours; that besides, we were not the first that had landed at the Mission of San-Joseph. The master, whom we appealed to, was of my opinion; he told us that indeed the landing would be more difficult and tedious at this place than at San-Barnabé, but that he believed he could answer for the safety of the ship and passengers. In consequence of this decision, which he gave us under his hand, it was determined

that

that we should land at San-Joseph. We accordingly cast anchor the 19th of May, half a league from the coast, opposite the mouth of the little river belonging to that Mission. But though we were at the end of our voyage, we were by no means at the end of our fears. A fresh gale sprung up from the east. A fortnight sooner, this wind would have been of service to us, but now it was very dangerous, and we were afraid of being stranded upon the coast. Mr. Doz and Mr. Medina begun to upbraid me with having insisted upon landing at San-Joseph, and so did the pilot. This wind, they said, would have been for us in the bay of San-Barnabé. It is an easy matter to judge by the event; besides, the day before, I had simply proposed my opinion, and these gentlemen, no doubt, thought it a good one, or they would not have agreed to it. The event vindicated me in my turn; for the wind abating,

abating, we got and eagerly seized a favorable moment for landing.

The pilot immediately sent out the long boat, to reconnoitre the coast, and to look out the most convenient place for landing. I durst not venture my instruments in this first attempt, and only put some of my small effects into the boat. They landed them with great ease. I then sent away my most material instruments by the second turn, along with Mr. Pauly and Mr. Noel, and reserved myself for the third. The second landing was not so successful as the first: Mr. Pauly wrote me word from the water-side that they had been in great danger, the boat having been several times under water, but happily they came off with no other harm than their fright, and being very wet, as were all the chests. This last circumstance made me extremely cautious in removing my clock, which I had kept by me, and for which I dreaded

the

the sea water. I therefore wrapped it up very close, and sat down upon it myself, to keep it dry in case the waves should chance to wash us.

Our fate now depended entirely upon the dexterity of the master, and the exactness of the sailors in executing the maneuvre. In the two former turns, they had marked the track we were to keep, by means of a buoy, or floating cask. Our master, with his eye fixt upon this mark, guided the boat that way, through a multitude of billows, which with a horrid roaring dashed against the shore, or amongst rocks all covered with foam. The sailors on their part, attentive to the word of command, now rowed with all their might, now again stood stock still, either to avoid a wave ready to break over the boat, or to keep in the way of another that might waft us ashore. It was by this maneuvre, executed with the utmost dexterity and success,

success, that at last we got safe to land on the coast of California, at the entrance of the river of San-Joseph. Night was coming on; so, determined not to go to San-Joseph till morning, I laid me down by the water-side. Then it was, that casting my eyes upon my instruments that lay all round me, and not one of them damaged in the least, revolving in my mind the vast extent of land and sea that I had so happily compassed, and chiefly reflecting that I had still time enough before me, fully to prepare for my intended observation, I felt such a torrent of joy and satisfaction, it is impossible to express, so as to convey an adequate idea of my sensation.

The news of our arrival soon reached the mission of San-Joseph; they directly sent us mules. I went thither, leaving Mr. Pauly by the water-side to look after the baggage, which I could not carry away, but which was brought me the next

next day. I made haste to establish myself at San-Joseph, and to prepare for my preliminary observations. Myself and all my train took up our abode in a very large barn. I had half the roof taken off towards the south, and put up an awning, that could be spread out or contracted at will. All my instruments were fixed just as they were to stand to observe the transit of Venus. The weather favoured me to my utmost wish. I had full time to make accurate and repeated observations for the setting of my clock. At last came the third of June, and I had an opportunity of making a most complete observation.

Doubtless the reader will see with concern that Mr. Chappe's account ends here, where it would have been most interesting, by the informations he might have given us, relating to California; but here, as in many other places, it has
not

not been in my power to supply the want of the author's own account; those who attended him not being able to give me any distinct information. All they have retained of that fatal country is the melancholy event of Mr. Chappe's death; what they have related concerning it is this.

An epidemical distemper raged at San-Joseph, and had already swept away one third of the inhabitants, when Mr. Chappe came thither. They might have escaped the contagion by going on to Cape San-Lucas, and this was what the Spanish officers proposed, but they were within a few days of the transit, and a second removal would have lost them some very precious moments. Mr. Chappe, less apprehensive of endangering his life than of missing the observation, or making an imperfect one, declared he would not stir from San-Joseph, let the consequence be what it would.

In

In the mean time, the numbers that were daily carried off, too plainly shewed the danger he was in, but every day brought him nearer to the object of his wishes, and Mr. Chappe cared for nothing else. The joy he felt when they were accomplished, was soon damped by the mournful spectacle to which he was witness.

On the 5th of June, two days after they had observed the transit of Venus, Mr. Doz, Mr. Medina, and all the Spaniards belonging to them, to the number of eleven, sickened at once. This occasioned a general consternation; the groans of dying men, the terror of those who were seized with the distemper, and expected the common fate, all conspired to make the village of San-Joseph a scene of horror. Whoever was intimately acquainted with Mr. Chappe, always observed in him two leading sentiments, the love

love of glory, and humanity. What a situation was this for a heart like his! Almost the only one among them all, who was yet free from the infection, he delighted in affifting all around him, but too foon he was himfelf feized with the diftemper. Reduced to want that affiftance he had afforded the reft but juft before, not one was left that was able to adminifter it. Mr. Pauly and Mr. Noel had fickened before him, and lay at the point of death; the only trufty fervant was in the fame condition: in a word, every one, Indians, Spaniards, and Frenchmen, all were either dying or haftening towards death.

Mr. Chappe had brought with him from France a little cheft of medicines and fome phyfical books. In this emergency he was an occafional phyfician. He examined the fymptoms of the difeafe; then confulting his books, he endeavoured
to

to find out the proper remedies. But he soon found himself as much at a loss as those who formerly consulted the oracles, whose ambiguous answers frequently admitted of two opposite meanings, and left them as much in the dark as before. Mr. Chappe had a violent pain in his side, and was delirious at times; in this case his books recommended bleeding, but then they expresly forbad it, and advised purgatives, where the distemper proceeded from a collection of bile. This was what he could not distinguish. Mr. Chappe, at all events, determined for purgatives. In the intervals of the paroxysms, he was forced to prepare his own medicines; he durst not trust the only healthy man among them, because a few days before, he had like to have poisoned Mr. Noel, by mistaking one drug for another.

Such was Mr. Chappe's dreadful situation. After three succeffive fits in three days,

days, he took two doses of physic, and found himself greatly relieved. But too much emboldened by this success, spurred on by a blameable, because an imprudent zeal, he would needs observe the eclipse of the moon the 18th of June, the very day he had taken his second physic.

It will be matter of admiration to look over the account of this observation. It is inconceivable how Mr. Chappe, low as he was, labouring under his malady, weakened by the fever fits he had gone through, could lend as close an attention to this phænomenon, as the ablest observer could have done in full health. Indeed he had much ado to hold out to the end of the observation. He was taken with a fainting fit, and a pain in his head, which continued till his death. The strength of his constitution still held out, but this only served to prolong his sufferings. He desired to be let blood;

his

his interpreter, a surgeon who had never practised much, and who was himself sick, tried to bleed him, but missed; however, encouraged by Mr. Chappe, he tried again, and succeeded. This did but encrease the disorder. In the evening he complained of an obstruction; he tried to ride out on horseback, and found himself rather easier; but soon after, his fever returned, and he lay in a most deplorable condition; suffering the sharpest pains, and destitute of all assistance. The village of San-Joseph was by this time a mere desert: three fourths of the inhabitants were dead, and the rest had fled to seek a less infectious air; but the contagion had already spread far and wide. Thus totally forsaken did Mr. Chappe spend his last moments. He expired on the first of August, surrounded with Mr. Pauly, Mr. Noel, and the rest of his attendants; but they were all so languid, that they had hardly strength

strength to crawl to him, and reach out their arms to catch his laſt breath.

Mr. Chappe ſaw death approaching, with the ſteadineſs and ſerenity of a true philoſopher. The intent of his voyage was fulfilled, and the fruits of his obſervation ſecured: he ſaw nothing more to wiſh for, and died content. The public and his friends are the only loſers by his death. Their tears are the beſt encomium on his memory, and the moſt flattering reward of his labours. The reader will doubtleſs ſhare them at the recital of ſo affecting a ſcene.

Mr. Doz and Mr. Medina did their beſt to pay their laſt reſpects to Mr. Chappe. The prieſt or miſſionary of San-Joſeph was long ſince dead, as were almoſt all the inhabitants. The Spaniards, the French, and every one of the ſurvivors, then collected what little ſtrength they had

had left, and performed the moſt melancholy of all offices, and this cruel moment rouſed all their fears, with the dread of the like tremendous fate. Of the Spaniards, Mr. Medina was in ſuch a weak and languid ſtate, as left him little hopes of ſurviving Mr. Chappe much longer. Of the French, Mr. Dubois was not leſs dangerouſly ill. As for Mr. Doz, Mr. Pauly, and Mr. Noel, they were recovering apace. Though they were all impatient to get away from San-Joſeph, they were forced to wait there two months longer for the veſſel Mr. Chappe had been promiſed from San-Blas, to fetch and carry them over to Mexico. Even the ſick did not more ardently wiſh for the recovery of their health, than for the arrival of that ſhip. At laſt we were told ſhe was come to an anchor over againſt St. Ann's, in the little bay of *Ceralvo*. Mr. Doz and Mr. Medina, with all their attendants, except three that were dead, went

went therefore to St. Ann's, together with Mr. Pauly, Mr. Noel, and Mr. Chappe's servant. As to the poor watchmaker, he was not in a condition to be removed. They left him at San-Joseph, recommending him to some Indians who still remained in the place, in case he should recover. Mr. Pauly however, a few days before he embarked, sent to fetch him if it was possible to remove him, but he was no more. No doubt the grief of seeing himself forsaken in an unknown country haftened his death. Our travellers had now nothing more that could detain them in California. They crossed the Vermeille sea, where they met with very stormy weather, and were in real danger, but landed at last at San-Blas. There Mr. Medina found himself exceedingly ill. He had been very low from the first moment he was taken ill at S. Joseph. The fight of Mr. Chappe's death, the fatigue of removing to St. Ann's, and then
crossing

crossing the sea, had made him worse, and brought him to his grave. He died soon after the departure of Mr. Doz, who was obliged to leave him, and to go to Mexico.

Mr. Medina, having shared the dangers, the labours, and the unhappy fate of Mr. Chappe, well deserves to share with him the encomiums and regrets of the public. The Spanish astronomers were not less successful than Mr. Chappe in their observation of the transit of Venus. He on one side, and they on the other; they vied with each other in exerting their utmost care and skill in the observation of that phænomenon. A noble emulation kept them asunder at that moment, to dispute a success which could only turn out to the benefit of the public. May the competition of nations never propose any other end!

NATU-

NATURAL HISTORY

OF THE

PROVINCE

OF

MEXICO.

Extract of a Letter from Mexico addressed to the Royal Academy of Sciences at Paris, by Don Joseph Anthony de Alzate y Ramyrez, now a Correspondent of the said Academy, containing some curious particulars relative to the Natural History of the Country adjacent to the City of Mexico [1].

GENTLEMEN,

THE departure of Mr. Pauly for Paris procures me a favourable opportunity of sending you several of the curiosities of

[1] This letter, written in Spanish, was delivered to the academy by Mr. Pauly, together with Mr. Chappe's papers: Mr. Pingré was desired to translate it into French, in order to its being read at one of their private meetings. Every thing is here left out that is foreign to natural history, or of little or no consequence to the public.

this country*. I think it will not be amiss to subjoin an explanation, which however I submit to your judgment and learning.

I have been greatly affected by Mr. Chappe's death. New Spain has lost in him a man whose talents would have been of great service, to make known a thousand natural curiosities which here lie buried in oblivion. Those who are fittest to rescue them from it, either disregard them, or are not able to communicate them to the public.

* The chest containing the specimens of natural history, mentioned here by Don Alzate, did not come to hand till long after this letter. The academy then appointed M. de Jussieu and M. Fougeroux de Bondaroy to examine them, and to make their report. Mr. Fougeroux has favoured me with his observations on the specimens, and has given me leave to insert the following notes, for the better understanding of Don Alzate's letter.

By

PROVINCE of MEXICO.

By what I can collect from Mr. Pauly's account, Mr. Chappe must have died of an epidemical distemper, which we call here, in the Mexican language, *Matlazahualt*, but at Vera Cruz, Carthagena, and elsewhere, goes by the name of the black vomit. This distemper is the scourge of Mexico. In 1736 and 1737 it swept away above one third of the inhabitants of the capital; and in 1761 and 1762, it made yet greater devastations, and depopulated this kingdom. At least twenty five thousand died within the walls of this city; it is true this time, beside the contagious distemper, an epidemical small-pox raged here, which contributed not a little to the havoc that was made.

The Matlazahualt seems to me to proceed entirely from the bile mixing with the blood. Those who are seized with it look pale, and most of them bleed at the nose

nose and mouth, which happens when a crisis is coming on[7]. A relapse is more dangerous than the first, and most of the sick do relapse. In the contagion of 1761, (the only one I have had an opportunity of observing, as I was born during the course of the former.) I took notice that purgatives and bleeding were very dangerous, insomuch that persons who were let blood or took physic for other disorders, were directly seized with the Matlazahault. This disease chiefly attacks the Indians, and always begins by them. In 1761, above nine thousand patients were admitted into the Royal Hospital (which is only for Indians) in the space of twelve

[7] Mr. Chappe had no vomiting. His complaints were violent fever fits, great pains in his head, a load upon his chest, which he called an obstruction. This by no means answers to the description given here by Don Anthony de Alzate.

months,

months, and no more than two thousand recovered.

Few plants afford such botanical curiosities as the *Maize*, or Indian corn. It shews in the clearest manner, and with the greatest certainty how the seed feeds in the plant, and how, when the grain is replenished, the plant remains insipid, and consequently that the juices it contained at first, have been exhausted to nourish the seeds, after they had been brought to perfection in the plant. This is so true, that the plants of maize that bear no seed, (and these are very numerous here) are always extremely sweet. They are brought to market at Mexico, and the children are as fond of them as they are of sugar canes, and indeed they call them *canes*. I have pressed some of these plants, and boiled up the juice, and it actually yielded real sugar. In Mexico, when they have sowed the maize, they let it grow without

out any culture, and then it turns to canes, and bears no fruit at all.

Though several authors have given very good descriptions of the *Maguey*, the plant from which they draw the *pulco*, a kind of drink which supplies the want of wine, I think none has taken the pains to enquire what quantity of liquor may be extracted from this plant[1]. A Maguey will yield two *arobes* of liquor in the four and twenty hours, and continues to yield as much every day for six or eight months together[2].

I send you likewise a simple, which I think the best that has hitherto been used

---

[1] The inhabitants of Xachimilco understand best how to cultivate the Maguey, and it grows larger there than any where else.

[2] The arobe is about twenty-five pounds, so that we may reckon at the rate of four arobes to the hundred weight.

for dying in black. It is called *Cafca-lotte*[10]. It is a large tree, and grows only in very hot countries. The leaf is small, and very much resembles the *Huifiache*, which I shall speak of next. It bears a yellow flower. The growth of this tree is as slow as that of the oak, or flower. I need not describe the fruit, as I send you a specimen of it. Galls are not to be had here but at the apothecaries; they make use of them in their medicines, and get them from Europe. We could not dye

---

[10] The cafcalotte is a species of acacia; its fruit is a long and broad pod, often crooked: it confifts of a thin woody fhell, covered over with a thick rind. It is a little reddifh on the outfide, and when dry, is eafily reduced to a fine powder. The pod contains many flattifh feeds, of a light and bright yellow.

It is well known that the pods of almoft all the acacias yield a black colour; they may likewife be ufed in the tanning of leather. Sloane fays the acacia indica is ufed in making ink. (Hift. Jamaica.)

black here, if nature had not furnished us
with the cafcalotte. The dye that is
procured from this fimple is better, becaufe
lefs corrofive, than any other; and indeed
black is moft generally worn here, as it
has been found by experience to be the
moft lafting. Even the moft common
hats lofe nothing of their firft luftre, and
wear all to pieces without the leaft alteration in their colour.

The *Huifiache*" is likewife ufed for
the black dye, but it is not fo good as
the Cafcalotte. Its chief ufe is for ink.
This tree requires warmth, yet they have
the bad cuftom of planting it in a cold
foil, fuch as that of the town of Mexico,

" The *Huifiache* is likewife a kind of acacia, not unlike the *Inga* or fugar pea of America, defcribed by feveral botanifts. The fhell of this pod is hard, thick, and black; it contains feve- ral feeds, each in its own cell, the fhell being di- vided into fo many partitions.

where there are seven growing, besides those that are within the enclosure of the baths.

I send you an exact drawing of the monstrous tree of Attisco, called *Abuehuete*; its dimensions are taken with the greatest exactness. This tree is always extremely large. I send likewise some of the seed or nut, and the leaf[t].

Now

[t] The figure of this tree, sent by Don Alzate, affording no criterion whereby to ascertain its species, I have had recourse to the fruit and a leaf, which were found in the same parcel, and upon inspecting them, I am of opinion they may belong to the *cupressus lusitanica patula, fructu minori*. (Inst. page 587.)

The fruit is made up of scales, and the seeds within are placed as in the pine apple; so that it must be a true cypress, no way like the *cupressus foliis acaciæ deciduis*, in which every scale of the fruit covers a kernel. Beside, the leaf found with the seeds of the mexican tree is made up of little leaves, that are not opposite, as in the acacia-leafed cypress. It results therefore from this

exami-

Now that I am upon the topic of monstrous trees, it will not be improper to mention the *sabino*, which stands in the church-yard of Popotta, a village about half a league from Mexico. Its trunk measures sixteen *vares* and a half round. (Our vare is not quite three feet [1].)

There is another tree in the yard of the parsonage house, which exhibits a singular phænomenon. It is customary to tie the horses to one of the boughs, so that the bark is all stript off, and nothing is seen but the bare wood. Notwithstanding this, the branch preserves its verdure, and bears

examination, that the tree Don Alzate speaks of is not the acacia-leafed cypress; nor is it that of Portugal, though the ahuehuete really resembles this in its fruit. It is therefore a new and undescribed species of acacia, and which would necessarily come into the genus of cypress.

[1] The trunk of this tree must then measure about fifty feet in circumference.

fruit just as if the bark was on. It is a fine tree, and bears very pleasant fruit. It is what we call *sopote blanco*.

I send you a seed of what we call *Chia*; we put it to infuse for a couple of hours, sweeten it with sugar, and drink the liquor. It is from this seed that we extract the oil which our painters use for mixing their colours, and which gives our pictures such a beautiful gloss: perhaps in time it may be put to some other use. The way they draw the oil is by roasting the seed, and then pressing it [14].

I recollect a plant which I believe has not its fellow amongst the known plants,

---

[14] The seeds sent us by Don Algate belong to the plant which Linnæus calls *Salvia Hispanica*. This seed is come up here, and we have long had the very same plant. The Italians cultivate it too. Mr. Harduisii has given a description of it with a plate.

I mean the *Cacabuate* [15]. We know of many plants that feed us by their roots, but that a plant should produce its fruit in the very root, is, I think, a property peculiar to this I am speaking of. I send you the plant and the fruit, and will tell you how it is cultivated. It is sown in hot countries, and will succeed in the temperate. They sow the fruit at a foot distance, and let the plant stand till it is about half a foot high; then they bury that branch (which they call *Fiſtolillo*) so as that both extremities, the root and the top, lie under ground till it is gathered in.

---

[15] This plant is the *Arachinna*, or *Arachis*, of Linnæus, an American ground piſtacho. It bears a pod which is very tender and brittle, especially when it is dry. Within this pod are two almonds of a very pleaſant taſte, which gives them the name of ground piſtachoes. It is common in all the hot countries of America. It has been raiſed here in hot houſes, and has borne fruit. It ſinks its piſtil into the ground, and there the fruit ripens.

PROVINCE OF MEXICO. 89

At harvest time, they pull up the branches of the plant to take off the fruit, which is found in great plenty. Though they do not sow it over again, the field will always yield a fresh crop from what was left behind. It is incredible what quantities are consumed in this kingdom, especially for their collations. They roast it over a slow fire to prepare it for eating. It is also put to other uses to supply the want of almonds. This fruit is unwholesome, and particularly hurtful to the throat. I must observe here that the plant bears its fruit, not in the original root, but at that end which was turned down into the ground. I must add one circumstance more, which is, that this plant appears beautiful when the sun shines, but withers when it withdraws.

I send you some viviparous scaly *fishes*, of which I had formerly given you an account". What I have obferved in them this year is—" If you prefs the belly with your fingers, you force out the fry before their time, and upon infpecting them through the microfcope, you may difcern the circulation of the blood, fuch as

"Don Alzate has fent thofe fifhes preferved in fpirits; their fkin is covered with very fmall fcales; they vary in length from an inch to eighteen lines, and they are feldom above five, fix, or feven lines in the broadeft part. They have a fin on each fide near the gills, two fmall ones under the belly, a fingle one behind the anus, which lies between the fin and the fingle one; the tail is not forked; laftly, this fifh has a long fin on the back, a little above the fin, which is under the belly.

We know of fome viviparous fifhes in our feas, fuch as the loach, &c. moft of thefe have a fmooth fkin without any fcales. The needle of Ariftotle is viviparous, and yet covered with broad and hard fcales, I have caught fome that had young ones ftill in their womb. As to thefe viviparous fifhes, it is a particular and new fort, and we are obliged to Don Alzate for making us acquainted with it. It breeds in a lake of frefh water near the city of Mexico.

it is to be when the fish is grown up."
If you throw these little fishes into water, they will swim as well as if they had been long accustomed to live in that element. The fins and tail of the males are larger and blacker than those of the females, so that the sex is easily distinguished at first sight. These fish have a singular manner of swimming; the male and the female swim together on two parallel lines, the female always uppermost, and the male undermost; they thus always keep at a constant uniform distance from each other, and preserve a perfect parallelism. The female never makes the least motion, either sideways or towards the bottom, but directly the male does the same.

Amongst the singular *insects*, the black spider of this country deserves to be taken notice of. It greatly resembles, in shape, the tarentula of the kingdom of Naples.

It

It may be about eight lines long; it is hairy, and of an ash colour. It is never seen in the day time, and by night only in fair weather, but it forebodes approaching rain. It is an unerring barometer. This observation was communicated to me by a virtuoso, and I have never known it to fail. Whenever I have seen these spiders, the weather constantly changed to rain within four and twenty hours.

The *Mariposa plateada*, or silvered butterfly, appears to me, gentlemen, to merit your attention, as you have none of this kind, at least it is not described by Mr. de Reaumur[17]. The bags which I send

[17] We have naker'd butterflies, which only differ from those of Mexico and America in size. Ours are smaller, and somewhat fainter coloured; these varieties may be owing to the climate. The naker'd butterflies here spoken of, and ours are both diurnal butterflies. Mr. de Reaumur and Mr. Geoffroy have described the latter, and both say they are not acquainted with the caterpillar that

I send you are of a curious structure.
I do not believe any such are to be found
in

that produces them. It might be inferred from
analogy, that these caterpillars, being of the class
that produce diurnal butterflies, make no bean,
but that the chrysalis fastens to the boughs of
trees, and are there metamorphosed.

If Don Alzate's observation is just, and if the
naker'd butterfly he sends us really came out
of this singular bean, we might gather some
useful hints from this discovery. 1. As we have
found in these beans the cast-off skins of prickly
caterpillars, we might conclude that the naker'd
butterfly comes from a caterpillar of that kind.
2. Now that we are acquainted with the bean of
the naker'd butterfly of Mexico, we might the
better find out the bean and caterpillar belonging
to that butterfly, so common in our own climates.
But I have some suspicion that the naker'd butterfly, sent us by Don Alzate, did not really
come out of that bean which he sent along with
it, and it were to be wished this observation could
be further verified. The ground of my suspicion is, that Mrs. Merian has described the caterpillar belonging to this diurnal butterfly; she
looks upon it as one of those that do not turn
to a bean; and says, that the chrysalis is suspend-
ed like most of the same class. (See Insects of
Surinam, vol. i. pl. 25.)

However

in Europe. You can beſt explain how the little butterfly, when he is juſt born, opens the lid or door of his bean, when you have examined how curiouſly it is adjuſted. I get a multitude of theſe beans every year, and could never yet find out how the butterfly works itſelf out, nor by what induſtry the caterpillar weaves its ſhell ſo ſkilfully, nor yet how the ſilks, being of ſuch a glutinous texture, do not cling together before the work is completed. I have much to ſay concerning our butterflies, but it ſhall be for another opportunity.

I think I told you, gentlemen, in a former letter, that I did not know of any petrifactions in this kingdom. I have ſince been informed there are ſome in a

---

However this be, the bean ſent by Don Alzate will ſtill be a curioſity, on account of the lid which the inſect contrives, and which he lifts up at will.

little

little place called *Chalma*; I intend to go thither, to acquire a thorough knowledge of these petrifactions. I have seen some very precious shells which were found at *Souvra*; they are of the same matter that is used for extracting silver and gold. I have been assured that in digging a mine in the province of *Roucra*, they found petrified human bodies, out of which they extracted a great deal of silver; among others the body of a woman holding her child in the attitude of suckling. The two bodies are perfectly petrified, and have yielded a considerable quantity of silver. As this relation appears to me to stand in need of confirmation, I chose it should be certified by the deposition of eye witnesses, and have accordingly written to some persons of that province, and I wait with impatience for their answer.

I gave Mr. Chappe a grinder of such an exorbitant size, that it weighed upwards

wards of eight pounds, was above ten inches long, and the rest in proportion. What animal this tooth had belonged to, I am at a loss to guess. It had been given me as a giant's bone. All I can affirm is, that the enamel of the tooth was in a great measure preserved. A virtuoso of this country has in his possession a leg bone, which unfortunately is not entire; some part of it is wanting. The head of the femur measures a foot and a half in diameter. This bone was found near *Toluca*. The Indian of whom it was bought, made use of it to bar his door; this is no wonder, as the remainder of the bone is still above five feet long. I am told the priest of the village of *Tecali* has lately discovered some bones of an enormous size, and, what is still more surprising, he has found tombs proportionable to these bones. I shall carefully enquire into this fact, and shall transmit to you, gentlemen, whatever I can discover.

In

In your memoirs of 1744, mention is made of dead fish having been found in the wells of Mexico, in confequence of the eruption of a volcano at Vera Cruz. This whole ftory is deftitute of all foundation. All the enquiries I have made, have not procured me the leaft intelligence about it. Not a foul at Vera Cruz knows any thing of fuch a volcano. At Mexico, nothing can be found in the wells; there is one to every houfe, but they never exceed fix feet in depth. The water is found at three feet from the furface at moft, and moft frequently at one foot. How then fhould dead fifh be found there, when the very nature of the foil makes all fubterraneous communication impoffible

I fhall here take notice of a fingularity in the royal domain of the mines of *Pachuca*, in the immediate dependency of the department *del Salto*. It is a mountain

tain made up of stones of all imaginable shapes. Stones of any shape or size that can be wanted, are to be had there, ready cut, for the trouble of fetching, and lifting them off the heap. These stones are not in horizontal but in perpendicular rows, and such as is one of them, such, you may be well assured, are all those above and below it[*].

What I am going to relate, though not of the same kind, is perhaps not less curious. I mean a stone, how large I cannot tell, as the greatest part of it lies sunk in the ground. The outward surface is above three feet over; the colour that of black marble, except a spot, or rather an incrustation of a different substance fastened to it. The singularity of this stone consists in this, that the slightest stroke

[*] This stone seems to be the *basaltes*, the same with the Giant's Causeway in the county of Antrim in Ireland.

upon

upon it with the finger, causes a sound with long vibrations; they call it the bell-stone, from the great resemblance of its sound with that of a bell. It stands in the bed of a river that is sometimes dry, and which runs through the town of *Cuantla*, the capital of that district which we call *Ancilpas*, about eighteen leagues to the southward of Mexico.

The following is a fact which I am witness to, and so will you, gentlemen, for I send you some of the petrifactions of the royal domain of the mines of *Huajannato*, which are inimitably beautiful. All the stones that are taken out of one of these mines have this property, that in whatever direction you divide them, they always exhibit an exact imitation of a Cedar. It is remarkable that in some of these stones, that part which forms the image of the cedar is pure silver, and the rest

rest of the mine abounds in the same metal. This mine is known by the name of the *cedar mine*, both from the representation on the stones, and from a fine cedar tree that actually stands at the entrance of the mine [19].

The

[19] In the chest sent by Don Alzate to the Academy, we found a piece of silver ore, singular by the spatheux crystals it contains. These crystals consist of thin lamina of a beautiful white, and not very hard. When exposed to the fire, they calcine and turn to plaister. This plaister is very fine and white, but rather coarse to the touch; but we saw nothing that looked like a cedar. There is a silver mine in Peru, the ore of which runs into the form of a feather, or of fern, possibly the author had that in view.

Beside these articles, Don Alzate's chest contained other seeds that were worm eaten, and are not come up; fragments of plants that could not be known, and to which they have ascribed certain properties in that country. We likewise found some buds of a large magnolia, or tulip-laurel, called there *Yolofochil*. Don Alzate says this flower emits a very fragrant smell, even when it is dry, and that the tree on which it grows

thrives

PROVINCE of MEXICO.

The natural vitrifications, which the Indians call *pelistes*, are to be found all over the kingdom. They abound at Mexico, chiefly in the northern part, but the place where they are found in the greatest plenty is the village of *Zuiapequaxo* near *Vailadolid*. There are whole mountains of it in that part. Hence the village takes its name, which is that given to

thrives best in hot countries, where it grows very large.

Mr. Noel, a young painter, who accompanied Mr. Chappe, has put into our hands several drawings which he took as they passed through Mexico and California. These drawings exhibit, in the vegetable class, a taper on which are found a monstrous excrescence, the flowers of a coral-ludendron, or immortal wood of America, and those of another plant, which we are unacquainted with; in the animal tribe, fishes, zoophytes, the sea hand, &c. a lizard, which we think a singular one, and is called a chameleon in that country, and a quadruped which does not seem to belong to any of the classes that are either described or known.

these vitrifications in the idiom of Michoacan ᵐ.

The woollen threads I send you are called in the Indian language *tocLomites*. They weave them into ribands. The Indians dye them in a method peculiar to themselves, and very different from what is practised in Europe. For that purpose they only buy the scarlet seed; the other ingredients they mix with it are very insignificant. Thus they dye all their woollen things red at a very trifling

---

ᵐ The vitrifications sent by Don Alzate to the Academy are, *un ioitir d's volcan*, a true glass, compact, heavy and black: it is the stone of Galinace of the Spaniards, and probably the true obsidian stone of Pliny. The largest pieces found in Don Alzate's chest are mostly three inches or three inches and a half over, and about three lines thick. His account shews, that there has formerly been a volcano on or near the spot where the city of Mexico now stands. The whole face of the country bears the marks of antient volcanoes, and no doubt there have been many in those parts.

expence. As to their method, they keep it an impenetrable secret ⁸¹.

I shall conclude, gentlemen, by a singular fact, which in my opinion is analogous to electrical experiments. On an estate belonging to the late Don Alonzo de Gomez, secretary to the viceroy, situate in the jurisdiction of *Singiuluca*, to the north east of the capital, at the distance of about twenty-two leagues, one of the servants was lame with both arms; whether he was born so or not, I cannot tell. He was employed in tending the asses. Coming home one night from the fields, he was overtaken by a violent thunder storm, and got under a tree for shelter. There the lightning

---

⁸¹ There is commonly no great difficulty in dying wool; it is not so with cotten. Yet even for dying of wool, some preparations are requisite, and it would be very odd if the Mexicans could do without them to dye these tochomites red.

struck him, and left him insensible for some time. He received no other hurt, on the contrary, when he came to himself, to his great surprise and joy, he found himself restored to the free use of his arms and hands. The fact is certain; I have it from a divine of undoubted veracity, who was eye witness to it, and his testimony is the more to be credited, as he is totally ignorant of electricity or electrical matter. He barely relates the fact for its singularity, without pretending to account for it.

Such are, gentlemen, the observations I have the honor to communicate to you."....&c.

" The letter out of which this extract is taken, was read before the Academy, and was heard with great attention, and found to be very interesting. We are farther obliged to Don Alzate for a very accurate map of Mexico, which he has delineated from the best accounts of such travellers as he is within reach of consulting in that country.

country. He has also sent us a map, drawn up in Cortès's life time, by which it is evident that in those early times they already knew California to be a peninsula, and the extent of it was as well ascertained as it has since been by later discoveries. Had this map been published in his time, it would have saved many disputes about California. The readiness of Don Alzate y Ramirez to communicate to us whatever might be interesting in a country so new to us, together with his talents and personal qualities, have deserved the encomiums, and excited the gratitude of the members of the Academy, who have testified their sense of his merit, by admitting him to be one of their correspondents.

VOYAGE

VOYAGE

TO

NEWFOUNDLAND

AND

SALLEE.

By Count Jean Dominique de Cassini.

VOYAGE
TO
NEWFOUNDLAND
AND
SALLEE,
By M. DE CASSINI.

TOWARDS the middle of May, 1768, I received an order from the duke de Praflin to repair to Havre-de-Grace, there to begin the experiments upon Mr. *Le Roy*'s time-keeper. The frigate *l' Enjouée*, on board of which I was to embark,

embark, was preparing to fail towards the end of the month, fo that I had but little time left to regulate the watches before they were fhipped.

I fet out from Paris with my father on the 20th of May, and arrived at Havre-de-Grace on the 23d. The weather being favorable, we began our obfervations the fame day. We were foon able to fet them nearly at the mean-motion; and by the 30th of May in the morning, after feven days obfervation, they were regulated, and fent on board the frigate. The detail of all thefe operations will be given in their proper place.

We thought to fet fail on the 30th of May, at the evening tide, but were prevented by contrary winds, for feveral fucceffive days. Thefe, and the infufficiency of the tides, detained us in the harbour

harbour till the spring tide of the new moon. My father returned to Paris, and I remained at Havre-de-Grace with Mr. Wallot (an active and ingenious young German), who had been induced by his taste for science to visit France, and whose fondness for astronomy had determined him to attend me in this expedition, and to assist me in my operations. We improved the time we were forced to stay at Havre, in making fresh observations, which fully ascertained the state of the time-keepers. At last, with the new moon, we again attempted to get out, but met with the same obstacles as before, and were very near being detained twelve days longer. The want of water was our chief hindrance, so that we determined to lighten the frigate, and by that means we got her out of the harbour, and clear of the mole of Havre on the 13th of June, at seven in the morning. We were obliged to anchor in the road till evening, to bring off our guns and ſtores which had been taken out. At ſeven we weighed anchor, and ſailed with a wind that was not very favorable.

We found it almoſt as difficult to get out of the channel as out of the harbour. For ſix days we did nothing but tack about from the French to the Engliſh coaſt. The very next day after our departure, the ſea growing ſomewhat rough, the freſh ſailors ſoon felt the effects of its motion. My ſickneſs happily went off in twenty-four hours.

During theſe firſt days of our voyage, I made trial of a new lock invented by Mr. Vallois. Before I left Havre, I had orders from the duke de Praſlin to add the experiment of this machine to that of the time-keepers. Theſe experiments did not laſt long; the ſecond time I tried this machine, the main-piece broke off, and

and was lost in the sea "; I then substituted a second, which I had taken in case of need; this again underwent the same fate. These two accidents made it impossible for me to pursue these experiments; which were too few to afford any other conclusion than this, that the

first

" This lock consists of two pieces: the one is a hollow cylinder or roll made of tin, eight or ten inches in diameter: within, are four tin wings or slanting sheets, supported by an axis longer than the cylinder: the second piece is a square box, in which is enclosed the wheel-work that puts the needles in motion on a divided dial.

This box is fixed on board the ship: you take a chain made either of rope or brass wire, and fasten one end to the wheel-work, and the other to the axis of the cylinder; this done, you throw the cylinder into the sea. As the ship draws the cylinder after her, the pressure of the water upon the inside wings, impels them with a degree of velocity proportionable to the swiftness of her sailing. This rotation of the cylinder communicates the like motion to the wheel-work, by means of the chain which unites them, and the needles being thus set a going, shew upon the dial,

I space

first thing the inventor should have attended to, was, to give a sufficient degree of solidity to the several parts of his lock, to resist the impetuosity of the waves.

The trial of the machines relative to the ascertaining of longitudes, was not the sole object of our voyage; the duke de Praslin had found means to adapt it to several purposes very useful to the navy. Beside the experiments on the *watches*, and the *lock*, we made trial of the *lozenges* for making broth for the sick, and of the *sea-water* sweetened after Mr. Poissonier's method. For my own part, I made use of no other water till we reached Cadiz, where the sea-coal failed us. This trial, together with those already made in several long voyages, demonstrates the

---

spaces calculated by the revolutions of the cylinder; whence, by means of a table, you ascertain the way the ship has made. When I made the experiment, it was the cylinder that came off.

wholesomeness of this water, and confirms the judgment passed by the academy.

It was not till after six days sailing, that we judged we were clear of the channel. We had no room to complain of this sea, which is sometimes very rough. It is true we were in the best season of the year, so that we had only the winds against us, but this is a sad obstacle, for nothing is so irksome as to be perpetually driven back from the track you want to pursue. We were sailing westward at a season when the winds generally blow from that quarter, yet, notwithstanding their obstinate opposition, in twenty-eight days we reached the eastern skirts of the bank of Newfoundland, commonly called the Great Bank. On the 9th of July we perceived by a mist that we were drawing near to that dreary coast. It rose in the morning: whilst it remained thin, the weather was very hot; at noon Reaumur's thermometer was at twenty-one degrees, the highest it had yet shewn; about one o'clock the fog thickened, the air grew cooler, and by three, the same thermometer was come down to thirteen degrees above O. The winds became very favorable, and drove us apace in a good track. This singular advantage did not last long, for at midnight the wind fell, and we had a dead calm till noon the next day, July 10.

As we deemed that we were very near the bank, we had kept sounding for several days past. At last on the 11th of July, at half past five in the evening, we sounded, and found eighty-four fathom. Whilst they were sounding, one of our sailors cast a line at a venture; it was hardly down before it caught a cod. The fish and the plummet came up almost at
the

the same time, and both confirmed our arrival at the bank ".

The bank of Newfoundland is famous for the quantity of cod that it affords, and for the fishery that is annually carried on there by the English and French, who are sole possessors of that branch of trade in those parts. This sand bank extends from the 41st degree of latitude to about 49½, and its greatest breadth may be about 80 leagues". Cod is generally found through-

---

" No cod is to be found in open sea; they always keep in the shallows.

" From about 49½ deg. of latitude to the eastward of Newfoundland, quite to the coast of New England, you find a succession of sand banks. That of Newfoundland, so called from the neighbouring island, is the largest of all, and indeed larger than any sand-bank that we know of, whether in the ocean, or in any other seas; it is therefore justly called the great bank. It is 80 leagues wide in the broadest part. However, the limits cannot be perfectly exact; for it is no easy matter to delineate a sand-bank upon a map, especially in a latitude where the sky will admit of taking observations.

out this immense extent, but the fishermen observe that the greatest plenty is commonly about that part of the bank which lies between the forty-third and forty-sixth degrees, especially towards the eastern shore. The vessels destined for this fishery sail from France from the end of February to the end of April. Happy those however who can get there by the middle of April. From that time till about the 15th of June, the fishery is most plentiful; after that, the capelans[14] going to deposit their eggs along the several coasts of Newfoundland, draw away the cod, which, pursuing after them, forsake the Great Bank, till the middle of September, when, still greedy after their prey, they are brought back to it by the same fish, which now forsakes the shore, and returns

---

[14] The capelan is a small fish, about the size of a pilchard, but somewhat rounder and narrower. The cod devours it greedily.

to the ocean. The fishery again yields almost as much in September and October, as it did in May and June. Many ships consequently go twice a year to the Great Bank, and employ the interval when the cod is gone to the coasts, in returning to France to dispose of their cargo, and recruit their provisions and salt. Few ships indeed, except those from Olonne [17], go twice a year to Newfoundland; the rest are stationed there for six or seven months together, and never come home till they begin to be in want of provisions, unless they have made a speedy and plentiful capture, which is seldom the case. The fishermen all complain that the fishery grows worse and worse. Before, and after the war of 1744, prodigious shoals of cod flocked to the bank of Newfoundland,

[17] The principal ports in France where vessels are fitted out for the cod fishery are, Saint Maloes, Granville, Honfleur, Saint Jean de Luz, Olonne, and Bayonne.

and made the fortune of fishermen and privateers; but since the last peace, the produce of the fishery is reduced to one third of what it was before; doubtless because the bait of a small fortune has increased the number of vessels, and proportionably divided the profit.

The cod that is caught on the bank of Newfoundland, is that which is known in France by the name of green or fresh cod. It is salted on board the ship as soon as caught, and keeps in salt the whole fishing season, and till they return to France. The curing and salting of the cod, requires a great deal of care. The following is the method of curing and salting of the green cod.

As soon as the fisherman has caught a fish with his line, he pulls out its tongue, and gives the fish to another man, whom they call the *beheader*. This man, with a two-edged knife like a lancet, slits the fish

fish from the anus to the throat, which he cuts acrofs to the bones of the neck; he then lays down his knife, and pulls out the liver, which he drops into a kind of tray, through a little hole made on purpofe in the fcaffold he works upon; then he guts it and cuts off the head. This done, he delivers the fifh to the next man who ftands over againft him. This man, who is called the flicer, takes hold of it by the left gill, and refts its back againft a board, a foot long and two inches high; he pricks it with the flicing knife on the left fide of the anus, which makes it turn out the left gill; then he cuts the ribs or great bones all along the vertebræ, about half way down from the neck to the anus, he does the fame on the right fide, then cuts aflant three joints of the vertebræ through to the fpinal marrow; laftly he cuts all along the vertebræ and fpinal marrow, dividing them in two, and thus ends his operation.

A

A third helper then takes this fish, and with a kind of wooden spatule, he scrapes all the blood that has remained along the vertebræ that were not cut. When the cod is thus thoroughly cleansed (sometimes washed) he drops it into the hold, through a hole made for that purpose, and the *salter* is there ready to receive it.

He crams as much salt as he can into the belly of the fish, lays it down, the tail end lowest, rubs the skin all over with salt, and even covers it with more salt; then goes through the same process with the rest of the cod, which he heaps one upon another till the whole is laid up. The fish thus salted and piled up in the hold, is never meddled with any more till it is brought home and unloaded for sale.

It is difficult for one who never was there to form an idea of the life the fishermen live at the Great Bank. It must be as powerful

powerful a motive as the thirst after gain, that can prevail upon those poor wretches to spend six whole months between the sky and the water, in a climate almost always excluded from the sight of the sun, and constantly breathing so thick a fog, that they can hardly see from one end of the ship to the other.

This gain is sometimes very trifling, especially now, since the scarcity of cod at the Great Bank. The salt fish landed at Bourdeaux, Rochelle, or Nantz, sells dearer or cheaper, according to the plenty or scarcity of the capture, the time of its arrival, and the size of the fish. Those who are so lucky as to bring in the first cod, may make three hundred and sixty livres of the great hundred, which contains an hundred and twenty-four large fish. The second may be worth two hundred and sixty livres, but the last seldom fetches

more

more than fifty crowns. So much for what concerns the owner. As to the profit of the fishing sailors, it differs according to the customs of the port where the vessel was fitted out. At Olonne, S. Jean de Luz, and Bayonne, the crew commonly come in for one third of the lading; in other places, as at Granville, they have but one fifth; but every sailor, on his return, is entitled to a gratuity of one hundred to two hundred and forty livres, according to the dexterity he has shewn in fishing. Elsewhere, as at S. Maloes, the sailors are hired for the whole season, as high as four hundred livres per man. I do not think this a very good scheme for the owner; the fisherman, sure of his own profit, is less solicitous whether the fishery turns out good or bad, and consequently less diligent.

The

The cod fishery, independent of its utility in trade, of which it is no inconsiderable branch, is an excellent nursery for sailors. It has been observed, that the seamen who have been employed in this navigation, are more expert, more ablebodied, and fitter to endure hardships than others.

The very next day after we reached the bank of Newfoundland, the fog and the calm overtook us; this is the weather that commonly prevails there*. As the

---

* At and about the Great Bank, these horrid fogs infest the air most part of the year, and will last eight or ten days successively, sometimes longer. In autumn and winter they are not so frequent; but from the middle part of spring till December, they are almost constant: they are so thick that one cannot see at ten fathom distance. An incessant rain drops from the sails and rigging. The sea is seldom rough about the Great Bank. The sailors commonly ask those who come from the open sea, "*How is the wea-*
"*ther abroad*"?

calm

calm continued the whole day, we employed the time of this inaction, in fishing. The cod is caught with a harpoon fixed to a line; the best bait is that little fish mentioned above, which they call capelan; for want of this, they make use of the intestines of the cod itself. Though this fish is extremely voracious, it requires both custom and skill to allure him. We caught no great quantity, and though we were so many, the fish always went to the same persons, who were more dextrous, and consequently more lucky than the rest.

The fourteen days we spent from our arrival at the Bank to our landing, were one continued series of fogs, which made us very uneasy. The great number of ships that crowded about the Bank, kept us in continual apprehensions of running foul of some of them in the fog. Besides, having been for several days unable to observe

observe the latitude, we durst not advance, for fear of striking against the bars of Cape Raze[19]. Our charts placed us about the longitude of those rocks, and the computed latitude brought us pretty near them. These last days of our first run, were the worst we had yet met with, and indeed the worst of the whole voyage. Transplanted into a horrid climate, constantly choaked with fogs, we seemed to be forever excluded from the sight of the sun; nor could we hope to land, whilst this fog intercepted the coast. It was dangerous to go in search of the shore, even when the mist seemed to be dispersing. It is no uncommon thing in this latitude to see the finest clearing succeeded by a prodigious thick fog, and this within half an hour. Then the pilot repents

---

[19] These are sunken rocks, situated on the western coast of the Great Bank, in 46 degrees 20 seconds latitude, and about 54 degrees longitude.

his having approached the land, misled by the appearance of a clear sky, especially if he has not had time to take a survey of it; how can he get clear if the wind is not very favorable? What track shall he pursue to escape running aground? Such are the inconveniencies and hazards of navigation in the latitudes we were then in; and we were not long before we experienced how critical our situation was.

We only waited for the instant when the weather should clear up, to go and reconnoitre the land, from which we deemed we were not far distant. We thought we had at last attained the summit of our wishes. On the 22d of July, the finest sky imaginable filled us with hope and joy. The horizon, though not quite so clear as we could have wished, seemed nevertheless to promise a sight of land at five or six leagues distance. Upon the

the strength of this delusive appearance, we run directly towards the landing place, with a brisk wind; but how great was our amazement, when, without discovering any land, we suddenly perceived, at a small distance before us, the dashing of the waters, which could only be occasioned by the coast, or by rocks or breakers, which the fog concealed from our sight. No time was to be lost; we tacked about, and made all the sail we could to get away from a coast where it is dangerous being wind-bound, on account of the violent currents, which may drive the vessel ashore, if she has the misfortune to be becalmed [10]. Happily for us, the wind favored our flight, and

[10] The island of Newfoundland is surrounded with the most violent currents; they have no fixed direction, sometimes driving towards the shore, sometimes towards the main sea. This uncertainty requires the greatest caution.

we made for the Great Bank, there to wait till a less fallacious change of weather should permit us to go safely in quest of land.

This we had an opportunity of effecting two days after, by the finest weather imaginable. Nothing is more gloomy than the sky darkened by that thick and damp fog, as nothing is more beautiful than that very sky, when a north east wind drives away the fog, and exhibits a well terminated horizon. The sun was not yet risen, when the mist, which had been constant all the 23d, dispersed in an instant; a clear sky and a fair wind determined us to make directly for land. We set sail at two in the morning, at eight we discovered a small eminence rising in the most distant horizon. At noon the figure of this and several other points which appeared as we drew nearer, made us conjecture that the land we saw was

was the coast of Newfoundland, and that this first eminence was the *Red-hat*. However, we were still too far off to judge with any certainty, but at four in the afternoon, being but four leagues distant, we plainly saw we were not mistaken. The Red-hat, and in general the whole coast of Newfoundland, is very steep, and rises far above the level of the sea; we first discovered it at near sixteen leagues distance. The ships that sail in this latitude, commonly take notice of this mountain, its form being very distinguishable. It is said there are some spots from whence it really appears like a flapped hat.

We had steered toward the Red-hat till noon, the winds not permitting us to bear more to the west, and after taking the elevation of it, we were actually going to tack about, to get more sea room, when

when the wind shifted by degrees, and we made towards the island of Saint Pierre, which we discovered at six. Our first intention was not to anchor there that day, but considering how seldom we could expect such clear weather as we then enjoyed, we directed our course straight to it. About eight o'clock, judging we were very near land, we fired a gun for a pilot; we were answered. We fired repeatedly to shew our impatience, nor was it ill grounded. The wind was slackening more and more, night was coming on, and the weather seemed to threaten a fog for the next day. Our signals were indeed answered, but the wished-for pilot did not appear. We could plainly see the light of the guns that answered us, and by the interval between the light and the sound, we estimated the distance of the island, and

found

found to our sorrow that we were farther from it than we had imagined. To complete our misfortune, a calm came on, and for some hours we were afraid of being driven ashore by the currents; but the wind soon rose. Seeing no pilot come, we kept aloof, firing a gun every half hour, and each time we were answered by two. Never did a night appear so long; the weather was overcast, and foretold an approaching fog. At three we begun to suspect land, and about five we plainly distinguished the island of *Saint Pierre*, and particularly another little adjacent island, called the *Pigeon-house*, which lies at the entrance of the road. Having attained to this certainty, we tacked about, and sailed before the wind, steering for the Pigeon-house; we were still near five leagues off, and the fog was coming on. We spied a little boat making towards us; at first we were in doubt whether

whether we had best wait for it, but finding we lost sight of the land more and more, we determined to lay by, in case it should be the pilot. We were not disappointed; it was the captain of the harbour of Saint Pierre, who had been rowing about the island all night, unable to find us. He leaped on board; and was so perfectly acquainted with the place, that he did not mind losing sight of the land, and in a short time brought us safe to the entrance of the road. We had scarcely reached it, when the wind failed at once, and fell to a dead calm, so that we were obliged to anchor before the road of Saint Pierre, and then to tow the ship to the right anchorage. This laborious operation took us up from six in the morning till the next day July 26.

Thus after forty-two days sailing we concluded what may be called a pretty good

good paſſage, ſometimes indeed obſtructed by the fogs and winds, but this was no more than what we were to expect at that time of the year. We had met with no accident, no ſqualls nor ſtorms, and had almoſt always a fine ſmooth ſea ".

We were no ſooner come to an anchor at the entrance of the road of Saint Pierre, but a prodigious thick fog robbed us of the fight of the land that ſurrounded us, and this for two days together. Indeed one muſt have been ſix weeks at ſea, to lament being deprived of ſuch a proſpect as the barren coaſts of this road affords, and in general the whole iſland of Saint Pierre; but for ſeamen tired with the uniform ſpectacle of the ſea, the moſt hideous rocks have their charms; I was

". Only on the 2d and 5th of July, when we met with a very rough ſea.

therefore heartily glad to get on shore. The very next day after our arrival, I skipped into a canoe with Mr. Tronjoly and some officers, and we made for the coast, through the mist. Long before we reached the shore, an offensive smell made us sensible what we were to expect. The stench increased as we drew nearer, and was at the height, when we landed near a kind of wooden house, which projects into the sea, and is built upon piles. As our first business was to wait on the governor, we postponed our inquiries about this building and its use to another opportunity. We made the best of our way to the governor's house, through a field covered with nothing but white pebbles or flat stones, overspread with an innumerable multitude of cod. Mr. Dangeac, governor of the island, came to meet us with his family. They welcomed us with such politeness,

politeness, and during our stay there, were so attentive and obliging, that we were soon convinced that the delights of an agreeable society will compensate for the hardships of the worst of climates.

Mr. Dangeac was no sooner apprized of the object of my mission, but he made it his whole study to procure me all necessary conveniencies for my operations. I was loaded with his favours, and the manner of conferring them doubled the obligation. He compelled me to accept of the house, and even of the apartment where his sons lived. Accordingly I fixed my abode on the shore, with Mess. Leroy and Wallot; and the apparatus was set up, to be in readiness for the first moment of fair weather. I was so prepossessed that the sight of the sun was an uncommon phænomenon in these parts, that I was almost discouraged; but happily for us,

that

that was not the cafe while we remained on the ifland, for in ten days I had four which were fit for obfervations.

I fpent the intervals between my aftronomical obfervations, in furveying the ifland, and enquiring into the nature of the place, its inhabitants and trade.

The iflands of Saint Pierre and Miquelon are the only fettlements the French poffefs at prefent in this northern part of America, which includes Newfoundland and the coaft of Canada.

Saint Pierre is a very fmall ifland; its utmoft length may be two leagues. Miquelon is fomewhat larger, and may be about five leagues long. S. Pierre however is the chief place of the colony; the fafety of its harbour draws a greater number of fhips, and probably for this fingle reafon, reason, the governor has fixed his residence there"; for I am told Miquelon is a much pleasanter spot. They talk much of a fine plain, a kind of meadow, a league long, which makes a very pleasant walk. You have no such thing at Saint Pierre, where all is barren mountains, or rather craggy rocks, here and there covered with dry moss, and other weeds, the sad produce of a stony soil. I sometimes penetrated far into the island to acquaint myself with the place, and examine its productions; all I found was mountains, not to be scaled without danger; the lit-

---

[11] The fishing vessels are very safe in a pretty large *Barachois*, which answers the purpose of a harbour. What they call here *Barachois*, is a little pool near the sea, and only separated from it by a bank of pebbles. The road of Saint Pierre is a tolerable shelter for ships of burden, but care must be taken to examine the cables very often, otherwise they will soon be damaged by the stony bottom.

tle vallies between them are no better; some are full of water, and form so many lakes; others are encumbered with little sorry fir trees, and some few birch, the only trees that grow in this country, so far as I could find, nor did I see a single tree more than twelve feet high in all that part of the island where I went. The island of Miquelon is a little better stored with wood.

The most common plant I met with at Saint Pierre, is a kind of tea; (at least the inhabitants call it so) its leaf is woolly underneath, and it greatly resembles our rosemary, both in the leaf and stalk. There is another plant they call annise; I have tasted both, infused in boiling water, and think the annise is the pleasanter of the two.

Hence it appears how destitute the inhabitants must be of the necessaries of life,

in

in a country where no corn will grow, and where every the smallest article must be procured from France. They have fixed their dwellings in a little plain along the sea coast; they have small gardens, where, with much ado, they grow a few lettuces, that never come to perfection, but which they eat greedily when they are still quite green.

The want of pasture will not admit of breeding much cattle; fowls are the only resource as to meat. Their soups are commonly made with cods' heads, but I cannot commend them. If trade were open between this island and the coast of Newfoundland they would be in no want, but the English make a point to suffer no provisions whatever to be carried over to Saint Pierre, and all intercourse is strictly prohibited between the island and the main land. If at any time some English
ship

ship finds means to convey a few head of oxen or other cattle, it is by eluding the vigilance of a number of veſſels of their own nation, ſtationed there merely to prevent this contraband trade. Our arrival at Saint Pierre was celebrated by the death of a bullock; this was the nobleſt reception they could beſtow.

From this account, one would be apt to conclude, that the iſland of Saint Pierre could only be conſidered as a ſhelter for fiſhermen driven thither by ſtreſs of weather, yet we have made a ſettlement there. The iſlands of Saint Pierre and Miquelon were ceded to France by the Engliſh on the following conditions: " that no forts ſhould be built on either; that no more than fifty men of regular troops ſhould be kept there, difperfed on both iſlands; and that they ſhould have no military ſtores, or cannon, capable of making a defence." Accordingly, they are allowed but

but five or six small pieces of cannon, which are rolled to the water-side without carriages, and are only used for signals to the ships that want to come in. France, at the taking possession of these islands, appointed a governor. Such of the Canadians as did not chuse to become British were permitted to go and settle there; many went at first, but the difficulty of subsisting in such a barren country, soon determined them to quit it; the greatest part desired leave to remove to France; it was granted, but they were no sooner there, than they regretted the island of Saint Pierre and wanted to go back. A cargo of near three hundred arrived there just before us. Their unexpected return put the colony in some confusion; those who were left behind had seized upon the habitations which the others had forsaken; they had pulled down some of the wooden houses, and made

made use of the materials. The new comers were sent to Miquelon, which, with this addition, may contain five or six hundred inhabitants; Saint Pierre about half as many.

I observed above, speaking of the Newfoundland fishery, that towards the latter end of June, the *capelan* flocked from the main to deposit their eggs along the coast of that and the adjacent islands; and that then all the cod about the Great Bank came in shoals to these coasts: this is the critical time for the fishermen of Saint Pierre. The island is adjoining to a sand bank where the cod comes in great plenty. Whatever is caught there, is brought to Saint Pierre, where it is cured and dried. This is what is sold in France by the name of *morue seche*, or more properly *merluche*. Merluche or *morue fraicke* is therefore one and the same fish, only cured in a different manner.

Some

Some ships likewise bring the fish they have caught at the Great Bank, to dry at Saint Pierre, but these are few; most of the cod that is fished at the Bank, is brought home to Europe, and sold for *morue verte*, or barrel cod.

Immense labour and care are requisite for this operation of salting and drying the cod, though but an ordinary dish at last.

The manner of preparing and drying cod.

The cod intended for drying, is caught and beheaded in the same manner as the other, but it is cut up differently [*]. The *slicer*, instead of cutting the bones along the vertebræ only half way down from the throat to the anus, lays open the fish at one stroke, quite to the tail, all along the vertebræ, which he divides up to the throat, leaving each half of these vertebræ

[*] P. 120, &c.

and the spinal marrow in the flesh of the cod.

When the *slicer* has thus dispatched a fish, he drops it into a sledge that holds about half a hundred weight; a boy then drives the sledge to the place where the *salter* salts and spreads the fish of the day.

The *salter* lays down the fish flat with the flesh uppermost, and placing several of them side by side, he forms a layer of six, eight, twelve, or fifteen feet long, and three, four, or five broad; then he takes a great wooden shovel, about two feet square, and sprinkles salt all over the layer of cod. Care must be taken that this salt be laid on very even. When this layer is sufficiently salted, he spreads another over it, salts it in the same manner, and so on.

When

When there are large, middling, and small cod, they are kept apart, for a different depth of salt is requisite for different sizes. Too much salt burns up the fish, and makes it brittle when it comes to dry, and too little makes it greasy, and difficult to dry.

The cod is left in salt two days at least, and sometimes above a fortnight; then it is washed. For this purpose they load it on hand barrows, and empty it out into a laver not unlike a great cage, by the sea-side; there they stir it about in sea-water with paddles, to cleanse it from the salt and slime that it is daubed with, and when it is washed white, they put it again on the barrows, and carry it upon the gravel where it is to be spread. They first pile it up five or six feet high; the top of the heap terminates like a roof, that the fish may drain and harden.

Two, three, or four days after, as the weather permits, they undo the pile, and spread the fish upon the gravel one by one in rows, with the flesh uppermost. When it has lain thus in the morning sun, they turn it about two in the afternoon, the skin uppermost, and in the evening if they find that the wind and sun have dried them enough, they lay five or six of them one upon another, and a large one at top, to shelter them from the rain. The cod being thus disposed in little heaps, the skin upwards, they wait for the first fine day to spread them again on the gravel, first with the skin uppermost, and at noon they turn them, and when they have been thus exposed a second time to the rays of the sun, they are again heaped up, fifteen or twenty in a heap, and left till the next fine day, when they once more spread them upon the gravel. If after this they find the fish thoroughly dry, they place the small ones in round sharp piles like

like pigeon-houses, the middle sized in heaps of a hundred weight, and the large ones in smaller parcels. The former, when they have undergone a fourth sunning, that is, when they have been spread upon the gravel for the fourth time, are laid up in round piles; as to the larger ones, they must be spread in the sun five or six times at least, before one can venture to pile them up like the others. When they have stood so for three or four days, they spread them all at once upon the gravel in the sun, and then proceed to a new pile, laying the largest fish for the ground-work, the middle sized next, and the smallest at top; because the larger they are, the greater pressure they require, to squeeze out and throw off their moisture. This pile is left standing for a fortnight, and then the cod is again spread in the sun, after which the pile is erected once more, but reversed, so that what was at the bottom is now put at the top.

This pile may be let alone for a month, after which time the fish is once more exposed to the sun, and then piled up for the last time.

When all this is done, they make choice of a fine day to spread out these fishes, only an arm full at a time, and lay them on the gravel: they examine them one by one, and lay apart those that still retain some moisture; the dry ones are piled up, and the moist ones are dried again in the sun, and then put on the top of the other piles, that they may be at hand to be looked after, and dried again if they should want it. To conclude, the whole process, just before they are shipped, they spread them by arms full upon the gravel, to air and dry them thoroughly.

In order to ship this cod, they clean out the hold, and lay a kind of floor, either of stone or wood, on which they
place

place the fish, the first layer with the flesh uppermost, and all the rest with the skin uppermost. They dont fill the hold from one end to the other, without interruption, but raise several piles, both to keep the good and bad apart, and likewise to distinguish the different sizes of the fish. The large ones make the groundwork of the cargo, the middle sized come next, and the small ones are laid at top. They line the bottom and sides of the hold with small twigs with their leaves on, but dried first for several days. The cod being thus laid up in the hold, they cover it with sails, and never meddle with it more till they unload it for sale in Europe.

For these particulars about the curing of cod in the Island of St. Pierre, I am beholden to M. de R**, lieutenant of a frigate, who is perfectly acquainted with these matters, having been for a long time employed in that business on the island.

Slitting, salting, and drying the cod, are three distinct operations, the last of which is sometimes very tedious and difficult. The sun is seldom seen at Saint Pierre, and the want of sunshine is the loss of thousands of cod, which rot in the damps and fogs.

On the right hand of the harbor or road, is a house built upon piles in the sea; it is made of boards, and the roof of long poles interwoven; half this roof is covered with turf from one end to the other, and the remaining half is left open: they call this house a *chafaud*. This is the place where they slit and salt the cod. The floor consists of long poles, placed so as to let the intestines of the fish drop down between them into the sea. Half the roof is left open to let in the rain and fresh air, which carry off part of the nastiness and stench of the place,

that

that would otherwise be intolerable, and the fish is cured in that part which is thatched.

The fishing boats that are commonly employed in catching cod about the island, and bringing it to this *chafaud*, are small craft, with a square sail. The crew never exceeds two men, commonly attended by a dog, their faithful servant and companion. From their boat they shoot goelands and other sea-birds, with which they make their soup. The dog swims and fetches the bird, without any interruption to his master's fishery.

The most common birds on the coasts of Saint Pierre and Newfoundland are the *madre*, the *gode*, and the *calculo*. The eggs of the *madre* are white speckled with black; those of the *gode* are greenish speckled with black, and those of the *calcuco calculo* are brown with darker spots. These eggs are larger than hen eggs, and yet the birds are not much bigger than pigeons.

Behind the *chafaud*, appear the masts of shipping; these shew the situation of the *barachois*, where the fishing smacks are sheltered. This *barachois* is large, and tolerably fenced from the winds. It reaches to the walls of the governor's house, and may be about three hundred furlongs wide in the broadest part. It measures four fathom water till within twenty-five or thirty furlongs of the shore; however, it has some shallows where there is not above eight feet water, which must be carefully attended to. At low water you have not above five or six feet water over the bar that parts the *barachois* from the road. In neap tides you have nine or ten feet, but in in high tides, it rifes to fourteen feet. The tides are very irregular at Saint Pierre, from the variety of winds, and the different degrees of their vehemence; however, the fpring tides are commonly at the new and full moon about eight o clock.

In going into the road of Saint Pierre by the eaftern pafs, you muft beware of two dangerous rocks, called the *black-rock* and *baffe jaune*, the firft fituated eaft, the other eaft-fouth-eaft of the point of the ifle of Dogs, at about ⅓ of a league diftance: but they are only dangerous by night or in a fog; by day light you can plainly fee the *black-rock* above water, and almoft always the waves dafhing over the *baffe jaune*.

The great road begins at the little rock Saint Pierre; a fhip may fafely fail on either fide of this rock, and will find anchorage

anchorage in any part of the road within thirty fathom of the shore; but lest a side wind should rise, they commonly allow more room, and anchor at one third distance from the coast of Saint Pierre, and two thirds from that of the isle of Dogs. As to the south-east pass, where merchantmen commonly go in and out, it is much more difficult than the other, and is hardly practicable but for ships of two or three hundred tons burden at most. There would be depth enough at high water for frigates, but the pass is very narrow, as is likewise the channel that leads to the good anchorage. The pilot must be cautious of the rocks that lye near the *barachois*, some points of which advance under water into the channel, but may be avoided by steering nearer the shore of the isle of Dogs than that of Saint Pierre; he must likewise be careful to keep clear of the isle of Massacre, and of the innermost point of the isle of Dogs, where a

ship

ship might strike if she was to come too near.

The duke de Praslin's intention was that we should make no longer stay at Saint Pierre than was requisite for the verifying of the time-keepers. The weather proved so favorable, that in a week's time, I had a sufficient number of observations to answer my purpose. I soon informed Mr. Tronjoly that I had no farther need to detain him there. This news was received by every one with as much pleasure as I felt in imparting it. We were all heartily sick of this horrid country, and the expectation of that delightful climate we were going to, made us long to get there. I shall now briefly give the result of the observations I made in this first station towards verifying the time-keepers.

Before

Before we got to the island of S. Pierre, I had some suspicion that one of the clocks was a little out of order. The observations I made when ashore, plainly shewed, that which I called the second (from the date of its construction) had actually undergone some variation in our passage. I thought it must be owing to the damps and fogs we had been exposed to, at the very time when I first perceived that the clocks did not agree. Mr. Le Roy asked my leave to open the clock, that he might the better find out the cause of this disorder, which he was of opinion, must proceed from some friction, which was discernable by the ear, in the pieces of the machine. At first I would not consent, but fearing lest my refusal should deprive Mr. Le Roy of the surest means of discovering the defects of his work, and amending what might be amiss, I consented to the opening of the clock, which was done in the presence of Mr. Tronjoly, Mr. Wallot and

and myself. Mr. Le Roy stopped the movement, examined it a while, and found nothing apparently amiss; then, without touching it with any instrument but his fingers, he restored it to the same state with regard to the other clocks, that it was in before he stopped it. Mr. Le Roy gave me in writing the demand he had made of my consent to open and examine his time keeper, and I drew up a verbal process of the whole transaction.

The disagreeable impression this disorder of one clock had made upon my mind, was soon removed by observing the perfection of the other; not the least alteration had happened, and with regard to the mean motion it was, within a few tierces, the same as at Havre de Grace. This is very surprising after sixty days trial, and in such fogs as we had been exposed to [34].

We

[34] The verification I made on the island of Saint Pierre was not indeed absolutely compleat, the

We set sail the 3d of August, and got out of the road of S. Pierre at seven in the morning with a clear sky; there had been a fog the day before, and that was the last we had to encounter. A fair wind soon carried us beyond the Bank of Newfoundland; we lost the foundings August 9, to enter upon a finer climate. Clear weather, fair winds, a fine sea; such in few words is the history of our run from the island of Saint Pierre to Sallee, and makes any farther account needless. The melancholy inspired by the fogs and contrary winds in our former passage, was now exchanged for joy and hope, the effect of fair weather and favorable winds. We were not long in search of the coast of Africa, and came within

the longitude of this island not being exactly determined, but that equality of motion which I had observed in one of the clocks was a strong prejudice in its favor, which has been confirmed by the sequel.

foundings

foundings on the 26th of August at seven in the morning. The founding shewed we were not far from land, but a mist raised by the heat, prevented our seeing the shore; it disperfed at noon, and we then saw *New Marmora* at four leagues distance straight before us. We kept along the coast declining southward, to get near Sallee, which was now but five leagues off; but upon the moment of landing, we were stopt short by contrary winds. We then anchored near the coast, and the next morning we weighed, and came to an anchor over against the town of Sallee, at the distance of about a league to the south west, after a run of twenty-four days.

We foresaw some difficulties in landing, on account of the sand bank which lies acrofs the entrance of the harbour of Sallee, and durst not venture in without a pilot from the place. A xebeque from Provence

Provence lay at anchor long fide of us; her captain came on board, and the informations he gave us as to the fituation made us ftill more cautious. The next day after our arrival, a boat of that country coming to bring goods on board his fhip, Mr. Tronjoly fent an officer in a canoe, to fetch one of the moors, that he might guide him into the harbour, and give him an opportunity of waiting on the Conful, to get information about the country, and the manner in which we were to proceed. Mr. Tronjoly, chiefly attentive to the object of my miffion, in which he took all the part it deferved from a public fpirited man, and efpecially from a fea officer, zealous of his profeffion, enjoined this officer to enquire whether I might find accommodations for making obfervations on fhore. The meffenger fet off, and we were impatient to fatisfy our curiofity concerning a country that was fo new to us. We long waited to

no

ho purpofe; two days paffed, and no officer appeared, and we began to be uneafy "; however, he returned the fourth day, and told us the only thing that had detained him was the bar, which is fometimes impaffable for four or even eight days together. As to what concerned me, Mr. Cheinier our corful very obligingly offered me his houfe, but withal faid he would not anfwer for the impreffion that the fight of my inftruments might make upon a reftlefs and fuperftitious people. I could make no obfervations at Sallee without previoufly afking leave of the governor; he was therefore to be informed of the object of thefe obfervations, and then he could grant nothing till he had acquainted the King of

[11] We were the firft French King's fhip that had entered the port of Sallee fince the conclufion of a peace, which was not yet very firmly eftablifhed, with a people whofe honefty is rather precarious.

Morocco with it. All these preliminaries must take up some time, and we wished to make but a very short stay at Sallee; I was also apprehensive that once landed, we might be detained too long by the bar, and waste those moments here, which would be very precious elsewhere [34]. All these considerations put together, determined me to leave the watches and my instruments on board the ship: we even came to a resolution not to land at all, unless the bar should be smooth enough to admit of our coming back the same, or at farthest the next day.

The bar being practicable, some of our company took a trip to the town, but I

[34] The longitude of Sallee is not perfectly known. I could only have verified the time-keepers with regard to the mean motion, as I did at Saint Pierre. I wished therefore to get to Cadiz, where I was to verify them completely.

chose to wait till Mr. Tronjoly went, and to go with him. These first came back the next day; their quick return emboldened us to follow their example. Mr. Tronjoly, who wanted to speak with the consul, prepared to go on shore, and agreed to my attending him. Mr. Wallot was so obliging as to remain on board, to watch the time-keepers in my absence jointly with Mr. Le Roy, who had been ashore with the first company.

Mr. Tronjoly was impatiently expected by Mr. Cheinier the consul, and the governor of Sallee. They met us on the sea shore, surrounded with a great concourse of Moors or Salletines, who were eager to see us; they all shewed us tokens of friendship, and expressed by their gestures that they were not sorry to see us; they were even familiar, some taking us by the hand, others asking us for blan-

Llanquilles[17]. The whole time we ſtaid in the town, the governor, to free us from their importunity, and for fear we ſhould be inſulted, gave us a guard whenever we went abroad. This man, with a ſtick in his hand, walked before us, and without much ceremony, drove off thoſe who ſtood in our way; but this precaution was perhaps needleſs. We found the Salletines much more civilized and leſs ſhy than we had imagined. We met with nothing but marks of friendſhip from the principal perſons of the place; as for the common people, none but the little children ran after us, and abuſed us in their own language, but this we diſregarded, for we did not underſtand them. The word theſe children repeated ofteneſt was *bomba*, by which they meant to upbraid us with

[17] Small coin, worth three ſols four deniers French money.

the bombs that the French had thrown
into Sallee and Arache in their laſt expedition ".

We were to ſtay at Sallee only the remainder of that day, and to ſet off early in the morning, that we might get out before the ſea breeze ſet in. We ſpent that ſhort time in viewing the town, and the new objects it preſented both as to the place and its inhabitants. We were not much the better for this curſory ſurvey, but the next morning, juſt as we were to ſet off, the ſea was ſo rough on the bar, that no pilot durſt venture over. This continued the two ſucceeding days, ſo that

" In 1765, in the month of June, the French bombarded Sallee and Arache, and burnt ſome Salletine Xebeques: this expedition occaſioned a truce, which was concluded in October the ſame year; and at laſt in June 1767, a peace was concluded between the kings of France and Morocco.

we were detained near four days without a poffibility of getting at the fhip. For my own part, I was comforted by the opportunity this gave me of examining things, of which I fhould have had but a faint notion, had I ftaid at Sallee but half a day.

The civilities we met with from the conful, made us amends for the little intercourfe we could have with the Salletines; his kindnefs in procuring us a fight of whatever might fatisfy our curiofity, and giving us an account of what we had not time to fee, made our ftay at Sallee very entertaining and pleafant.

The town of Sallee is fituated on the weftern coaft of Africa, in 34 deg. 4 min. latitude [30], and 9 deg. 6 min. longitude. It

[30] I had it not in my power to verify this latitude: as to the longitude, I give it fuch

DESCRIPTION OF SALLEE. 169

It is one of the most considerable towns of the kingdom of Fez, under the dominion of the king of Morocco. A river called *Guerou* divides it from east to west into two parts, distinguished on the maps by the names of Old Sallee to the north, and New Sallee to the south; but the latter is more properly called Rabath [40].

The mouth of the river Guerou forms a harbour for trading ships, between the two towns of Rabath and Sallee, but the entrance is difficult, on account of the famous bar, or sand bank, that extends

such as I was able to deduce by the time-keepers, from some particular observations, taken on board the ship, in the road of Sallee.

[40] Probably this name of Rabath, given to the south side of the town of Sallee, has induced some geographers to call the river *Rebeta* instead of its right name *Guerou*.

all along the coast of Africa, and against which the sea, beating with incredible violence, rises in such billows as are exceedingly dangerous to pass. The bar of Sallee is the worst of all. It requires next to a calm to make it passable; the least gale from the sea renders it difficult, and consequently the favorable moments must be seized to get in or out of the harbour. The one is easier than the other; for, provided the sea does not break too violently over the bar, you can easily get in, observing always to present the stern to the wave, which of itself will drive the ship into the harbour. It is easiest getting in at high water, for then the waves are not so furious. But to get out of port, the best way is to endeavour to be beforehand with the sea breeze, which may occasion a swell, and then it is easy to conceive how difficult it must be to keep the vessel upright, and to conquer

DESCRIPTION OF SALLEE. 171

conquer five or six great billows that follow one another with vast rapidity; the first lifts up the ship, the next whirls her across, and she infallibly becomes the sport of the others, which swallow her up, without a possibility of affording her the least assistance. Some fatal instances have made the natives extremely circumspect in passing this bar. I could almost tax them with being over cautious, if an excess of prudence was not excusable in such a case as this.

From this account of the bar of Sallee, it is evident that such a local inconvenience must be very detrimental to trade. A merchant ship of some burden, that draws too much water to sail into the harbour, must anchor on the open coast, where she is not very safe, and may be compelled, by the shifting of the wind,

to

forsake her station⁴¹"; so that much time is lost before she can take in her lading. If once the bar grows rough, all communication is cut off. The distance of the anchorage will hardly admit of two turns a day⁴², and each of these is very expensive, because the Europeans chuse to employ the natives and their boats, for fear of losing their own⁴³. The chief trade

⁴¹ The north west winds are very dangerous; a ship must not stay till they blow hard, to weigh anchor and get sea room. Towards the latter end of September and in October you have frequent gusts of southerly wind, that oblige you to remove from the road. It is customary in the road of Sallee to cast but one anchor, that the vessel may remove with greater dispatch in case of need; or else they only fasten with a grappling and a small anchor for fear the bottom should cut their cables

⁴² The best anchorage is about three quarters of a league from the mouth of the river, to the north west, leaving the tower of Assan to the south east.

⁴³ The captain of a trading vessel lost his long boat and his sloop on the bar of Arache, the next port to Sallee; and at Sallee, one of their own boats perished, and only a single Moor escaped.

that

DESCRIPTION OF SALLEE.

that can be carried on with the Salletines, is in oil, wool, honey, wax, and Morocco leather; they take nothing in exchange but warlike stores, such as ammunition, great and small guns, sabres, &c. but they prefer money to all commodities, are very fond of getting it from abroad, and suffer none to go out [*].

The bar may indeed be of some service to the people of the country, as it makes any approach to their coast extremely difficult; but then this very defence sometimes turns against themselves. We saw an instance of it during the fortnight we lay at anchor in the road of Sallee. A small xebeque, unable to get into

---

[*] French money is not current at Sallee; the coin of the country consists of gold ducats, worth 10 French livres; the ounce worth 13 sols 4 deniers; the flus, 24 of which go to a blanquille; and the alaqunis, of which 80 make but a blanquille.

the harbour, the bar being then unpaſſable, came to an anchor not far from us. We ſaw her make many ſignals the whole day; at laſt we ſent ſome of our people on board, who found her to be a prize that a Sallee rover had taken from the Portugueze, and was ſending in with a party of his own crew. The poor wretches, having met with contrary winds, and not coming home ſo ſoon as they expected, had been for ſeveral days in want of proviſions, and eſpecially of water. They made ſignals for immediate aſſiſtance from land, but in vain. Some boats attempted to ſupply them, but there was no getting over the bar, and ſo it continued for four days ſucceſſively, that the wretched crew muſt probably have periſhed for want, within ſight of the harbour, if we had not been at hand to aſſiſt them with all they wanted. Excepting

cepting this bar, there is nothing remarkable in the harbour of Sallee.

During my stay ashore, I resided at Rabath. I was told there was nothing worth seeing at Old Sallee, which is only inhabited by the lower sort, so that I had no curiosity to go thither. What I am going to say of Rabath, may however be applied to both towns, which I shall frequently comprehend under one and the same name.

The houses in Sallee are flat on the top; they seldom exceed a ground floor, and have no windows, or any light but from the door of each room; no ornaments either within or without, except in the houses of the foreign consuls; these have both windows and furniture. The Moors sit on the ground, and have no other carpets than mats, or cushions that they call *estourmis*.

There

There are two principal ſtreets in Rabath, which are tolerably wide; theſe are the trading ſtreets. The market is kept in one of them; there the country people bring all the neceſſaries of life. The ſtreet is lined with ſhops for different commodities and trades. The other ſtreet is almoſt all inhabited by ſhoemakers, who make what they call *baboucbes*; theſe are no other than ſlippers, and is all the Moors wear when they do not go barefooted. This ſtreet is covered all acroſs with a platform made of hurdles, or boughs of trees, to ſhelter the workmen from the ſun, which otherwiſe would annoy them in their open ſhops. All the other ſtreets are very narrow. The quantities of oil made at Sallee[a], together with the naſtineſs of the houſes and their inhabitants, cauſe a very offenſive ſmell all over the town. In ge-

[a] They make oil with olives, but this is only for exportation; what they uſe at home is drawn from the *argan* nut.

DESCRIPTION OF SALLEE.

neral, the whole makes a very mean and wretched appearance.

The town is surrounded with a long range of walls, pierced with several entrances, each guarded by a particular kind of centry, who has no other mark of diftinction than a staff in his hand. The walls are very high, but not the more solid. At some distances they are supported by square projecting towers. Of this whole circumference, which is pretty large, some parts are mouldering away, some look threatening, and the soundest part would hardly withstand a broadside.

The burying places are enclosed between the city walls and the sea; these take up a great deal of room, as the superstitious Moors never bury two bodies in the same place, lest they should disturb the ashes of their fathers; and to prevent

prevent so criminal an indiscretion, they mark every grave with a stone, as a warning to beware of digging on that spot. In consequence of this custom, all along the water side without the town, you see large fields stuck with these marks, which, at a distance, look like sugar canes, or some other productions of the country; and the more so, as the fields that feed the living appear more bare than those that enclose the dead.

The most curious things in these burying grounds, are some little square pavilions, about fifteen feet high, topt with a little dome, or with a very flat cap; the whole is white washed, which gives it the appearance of some place of note, especially when seen from the road at sea, where they attract the notice of strangers. These places are held in veneration by the people of the country. Each of these pavilions

pavilions is the tomb of some saint, to whose folly, devotion and blind superstition have erected a palace in the realms of death. I shall speak hereafter of this kind of saints.

I wish I could have given a description of the mosques of Sallee, but it was not in my power to get any information concerning them, either by my own inspection, or the account of others. I do not suspect the Moors of being ingenious enough to have decorated the inside of these edifices in a very elegant manner.

To complete this account of Sallee as far as I am able, considering the short stay we made there, I shall here subjoin, that the tower of Assan is within half a quarter of a league of the town of Rabath, by the river side. It is thought to have been built by the Portugueze. Its height may be about an hundred feet. It is about forty-fix feet fquare on the outfide. You afcend to the top of this tower by fuch an eafy flight of fteps, that it would be no hard matter to go up on horfeback. The brick arches that fupport thefe ftairs, begin to yield to the injuries of time, and the upper ones are almoft all fallen in. The walls are built with very fine ftone, and are feven feet thick. Within thefe walls is another fquare, containing one room in every ftory, each of which has an opening that looks out upon the ftairs. I fhould have taken thefe rooms for prifons, had I not obferved in one of them fome remains of paintings a frefco, in the manner of mouldings. The Moors make no ufe of this tower, nor have they any notion what it may have been intended for in former times.

DESCRIPTION OF SALLEE.

The tower of Affan is fituated at the end of a fpacious piece of ground, encompaffed with walls, but only the ruins of them now remain; it was probably the place where fome palace or temple formerly ftood, for the remains of feveral rows of pillars are ftill vifible, fome of which are partly ftanding. I was defired to take notice of the ftone thefe pillars are made of; this ftone, they told me, was taken from the water fide, where it is fo foft, that you may cut it with a knife, fo long as it is wafhed by the fea water, but when expofed to the dry air, it grows exceeding hard, and is excellent for building. The tower of Affan is the only antiquity obfervable in the neighbourhood of Sallee.

Below the tower of Affan, is a round tower, lower than the former, and pierced with feveral port holes; behind this tower ftands the old citadel, of which it makes a part.

part. This citadel is rather a heap of ruins than a fortrefs, yet any but the Moors might make fomething of it. Its fituation, juft at the entrance of the harbour, is very advantageous, its extent confiderable, for it would lodge four thoufand men with eafe. This citadel was built by the Portugueze; it is falling to decay, and the Salletines are too lazy to repair it. They have planted fome cannon on the tottering walls, which crumble now and then, and bring down both carriages and batteries along with them; you fee the broken pieces lying among the rocks where they have rolled down, and no body takes the pains to pick them up.

To the right of the tower of Affan, ftands a pretty high turret; this is a mofque, and the pavilion on the top ferves to give notice of the hours of prayer. Below this mofque there is a battery of
twenty-

twenty-two pieces of cannon, in better order than that of the citadel; and lastly by the water side, a new one of fourteen guns, almost close to the ground. This is the only one to be feared on that side. A good way from this battery, on the right, and by the sea side, is a small fort, defended by three or four guns; the vicinity of the sea has been fatal to it; for whether by a storm, or as some say by an earthquake, the rock on which it is built was split, and the walls separated. The rocks at the foot of this fort form a little creek, by means of which it is sometimes possible to have a communication with the land, when the bar makes the entrance into the harbour impracticable; but this is not to be hazarded without great caution. I took notice, as I went along, that out of fifty guns which make up the whole defence of the town of Sallee, not above twenty are fit for service. They are

are placed at random, without any regard to their different sizes, and mounted on such sorry carriages, that they would infallibly be shaken to pieces, if the guns were fired often.

Between the city walls and the sea shore, you see little pavilions scattered about; these are the tombs of holy musselmen, and the ground between them is full of land marks, that point out the graves of private persons.

There is nothing remarkable on the side of the river, but a little turret, which is also a mosque, and a handsome new battery of twenty-two guns, erected by the sea side.

Without the town are the gardens, lands and possessions of the inhabitants. The gardens are very extensive, for this

plain

plain reafon, the land is the property of the firſt occupier; each takes as much ground as he thinks he wants and can till; if he grows tired of it, he forſakes it, and goes and ſows in the next field, if no body has been beforehand with him. In general, there is no ſuch thing as abſolute property, all the land belongs to the Emperor; but in this ſtate of poverty and general want of land, every one thinks he has a right to ſeize upon the monarch's property, as long as his majeſty is pleaſed to make no uſe of it, nor to claim it, which happens ſometimes, when a favorable opportunity offers, and a piece of ground has been improved by the labour and induſtry of the ſubject. The greateſt ornament and riches of theſe gardens, conſiſt in great plenty of orange, lemon and cedras trees; they likewiſe produce large quantities of pomegranates and figs. Theſe trees are planted as in a nurſery; and, without

without any art, form pleasant groves, where you breathe a cool and fragrant air. These gardens likewise abound with water melons, calabashes, meringens, tomatoes, and other productions peculiar to hot climates. The orange tree thrives best in a hot sun, which alone can bring its fruit to perfect maturity; however, it requires watering, and water is scarce in Africa, as sometimes it does not rain for six months together; therefore, in the highest part of every garden, there is a well, out of which the water is raised through a string of earthen pots, which move up and down by means of a wheel that turns a millstone. The water is thus conveyed into a reservoir, from which issue several pipes, which, flanting downwards, are so contrived as to disperse it all over the garden, through simple drains under ground, each of them terminating at the foot of an orange tree. The oranges, lemons, cedras,

dras, and every kind of fruit and vegetable that grows about Sal'ee are excellent; in short, I know of nothing that is wanting in the soil, but the industry of the husbandman, who may be rewarded beyond his labour. It would be a great mistake to imagine that Africa, and its burning soil, must be but a vast track of barren and dry ground, unfit for vegetation. The interior parts indeed, by the account of travellers, are an immense extent of deserts and burning sands, but it is well known that the parts bordering on the sea are very fertile. A good will, and industry, are what the Moors are wanting in, and hence partly proceeds that air of drought and barrenness which prevails throughout their country.

The kingdom of Fez is one of the most fertile cantons of Africa, yet half the country lies fallow. Half a league beyond Sallee, it is almost a desert. Nothing is to be seen but immense and naked plains, unadorned with a single plantation; not one tree is to be met with on the roads that lead from one town to another, and the weary traveller finds no shelter from the scorching sun. He must carry tents along with him to screen him from the inclemency of the weather by night, and also the provisions necessary to sustain life; for he may travel through a vast tract without meeting one single Moor. These people, except in towns, do not live in houses; they have no fixt habitations; ever wandering about the country, they remove sometimes one way, sometimes another, live in tents, and with their families form themselves into little societies, or moveable villages, which they call *adouarres*. Those who thus inhabit the deserts, are half savages, make as it were a separate nation, and have little or no intercourse with the inhabitants of towns.

The

DESCRIPTION OF SALLEE. 189

The inhabitants of Sallee may be divided into four claſſes; the true Moors, the Negroes, the Jews, and the Renegadoes.

The Moors are ſubjects of the King of Morocco, born in the religion of Mahomet. The Negroes are natives of the ſouthern and middle parts of Africa, ſavages who have been made ſlaves by the Moors.

The Jews are that wandering people, ſo well known by their calamities, deſpiſed of all nations, never able to form one of their own, and deteſted by the very Moors, notwithſtanding many conformities in their outward worſhip; but ſuch is the fatality of their lot, that I verily believe a Jew is more deſpiſed and abhorred by the Moors than a Chriſtian. Nevertheleſs, there are almoſt as many Jews as Moors in Sallee, and notwithſtanding the
contempt

contempt with which they are treated, they go on exercising their talent of cheating; but they must be very cautious, for the least misdemeanor, if detected, would cost them a bastinado. If a Jew happens to stand in the way of a Moor, the latter will strike him with his fist, or hit him a slap on the face, and the poor wretch has no right to resent the affront as it deserves. A Jew who strikes a Moor has his hand cut off without any trial; if he had a complaint against the Moor, he might have carried it before the governor: it is true he would have stood but a poor chance at that tribunal. The Jews are not allowed to set their feet in the burial places. By way of distinction they wear a cap and a black garment; black is the colour to which the Moors have the greatest aversion.

The Renegadoes are Christians of different nations, who have embraced the religion

gion of Mahomet from various motives of interest; some having fallen into the hands of the Moors, have abjured Christianity to escape the miseries of slavery; others from laziness and a love of plunder, have been induced to associate with a people noted for both. These Renegadoes are for the most part worthless persons, who having rendered themselves obnoxious to the laws at home, found no safety but in flying into a country where they are out of reach. These miscreants are mostly Italians and Spaniards; the Moors have sense enough to despise them. I admired the answer of a Salletine, who had been long a prisoner on board the French gallies: We asked him how he came not to turn Christian; " a good Moor, said he, can, " never become a good Christian, and a " good Christian," (pointing contemptuously at one of these Renegadoes) " can " never make a good Moor." The Moors, however, are too happy in having these
Renegadoes

Renegadoes among them; it is of them they have learnt the little they know of ship building and navigation. Some of these Renegadoes are so base as to command Sallee rovers, and go a cruising against their own nation, and bring away their countrymen, loaded with chains, to deliver them up to the worst of slavery: but whatever obligations the Moors may be under to these apostates, they value them no more than they deserve, and will not acknowledge them as Moors; they never call them but by the opprobrious name of Renegadoes.

The usual dress of the Salletines consists of a long narrow piece of white stuff, which they call *eckque*. The men and the women wrap it round their body in a different manner. Most of the men wear it only round their waist, and leave their arms, shoulders, and legs, bare. This white

white habit makes the Moors look like so many statues; those who are employed in any work that requires freedom of motion, wear no eckque, but a waistcoat without sleeves, and large trowsers, that reach from above the waist down to the ankles. The Moors all wear the Turkish turban, which is a kind of white handkerchief, twisted, and bound round and round their forehead; the top of the head is covered with a red cap or caul. They let their beards grow, but cut off their hair: the women however wear their hair.

The women wear the eckque, as well as the men; they wrap themselves up in it from head to foot. They are not allowed to shew their faces when they go abroad; an opening or two are contrived in the stuff, or in the folds of the eckque, through

through which they enjoy the benefit of seeing every thing, without the pleasure of being seen, which is no small denial to the sex. The husbands are excessively jealous; their wives are always shut up within doors, and are not suffered to speak with any man but their near relations; you seldom meet any in the streets of Sallee, except a little before sun-set, when they sometimes go to pray in the burying grounds, but then they are so well wrapped up, that you cannot possibly see any thing but two large eyes, which rather excite than gratify your curiosity. The freedom of the Jewish women is quite a contrast to the perpetual captivity of the Moorish wives. They wear no eckque, and go with their faces uncovered. This only relates to the common dress of the Salletines; I saw no other worn, except by the Governor. The day he received us in form, he was not in his mandrilla, but

DESCRIPTION OF SALLEE.

in the right Turkish dress. As for the women, they are so little seen, that I had no opportunity of observing what other clothing they may wear under the eckque.

The police of the town is in the hands of the Governor; who is at once magistrate, judge, and sometimes executioner. In the morning he goes to the flesh market, which is kept by the river side. Whoever has a bullock to dispose of, brings it to this place, kills it, cuts off the best piece, and carries it to the Governor, who upon the apparent goodness of the meat, determines at once how many pounds the dealer shall sell for a blanquille. The rest of the day, the Governor rides about the town, mounted on a mule, and followed by a servant armed with a stick. If he meets with any one that is guilty of a trespass, he directly condemns him to a certain number of stripes, as many as he thinks proper, and his servant is ordered to inflict them upon the spot with his stick, unless Mr. Governor chuses to take that trouble himself, or if his arm be not too much tired with the business. The sufferer can get no redress, there being no appeal to any supreme court of judicature, and it is taken for granted that what he suffered he had well deserved. Capital crimes alone are reserved for the cognizance of the Emperor. The principle this prince goes upon is to punish by the amputation of the offending member. The culprit is brought before him, the crime is laid open, sentence is immediately passed, the executioner is any one who happens to have a knife about him. He performs the operation just as he pleases. It is easy to conceive what a poor wretch must suffer in the hands of such a bungler, who with cutting, sawing, and breaking, at laſt gets the limb off, and applies no other dreſſing to the wound, than a little ſtreet dirt, and then pours melted roſin over it. I have been aſſured many ſurvive this operation.

There is no other tribunal but the Emperor's, no law but his will; he adviſes with no one; in ſhort, he exerciſes the moſt unlimited deſpotiſm. From this account we may eaſily gueſs what muſt be the conſequence of a government founded on caprice, injuſtice, and cruelty, and form a juſt idea of the Mɔoriſh nation; a people void of induſtry or true courage, lazy, profligate, ſtupid, ſuch as vile ſlaves muſt be expected to be.

It now remains to ſpeak to that article which ſtruck me moſt in the ſuperſtition of the Moors, it is that of their ſaints. If among the meaneſt of the vulgar there is found some oddity, who either from natural defect or from affectation, has any thing whimsical or ridiculous in his behaviour, he is directly accounted a saint; all fall down before him, run to kiss his hand, and beg his protection; all from him is respectable; they court his friendship, dread his anger; his enemy becomes the enemy of the people, and frequently the victim of blind superstition*. The crafty saint, who perhaps has put on the appearance of madness, only for the advantage he reaps from it, grows more extravagant and more holy than ever; he then becomes more powerful, and all his wants are supplied; they let him take whatever he has a fancy for, and kiss the hand that robs them. It is astonishing how far the blindness of mankind will go,

* It would be in the power of one of these saints to cause any man to be stoned to death, who should chance to displease him.

and

and how great is the power of superstition, which can sometimes make them so inconsistent with themselves, and will silence their warmest feelings! Is it credible that the most heinous affront, reproach and injury that can be offered to a Moor, (whose ruling passion is the most furious jealousy) should be accounted by him a glory, a merit, an honor, when it is bestowed by one of these saints, who desire no better than to enjoy in this world the foretaste of Mahomet's paradise. The following fact is positively asserted: A bride, with her husband, and several persons that had attended the wedding, were crossing the river in a boat; one of these saints happened to cross over with them; he took a fancy to the bride, his holiness signified his will and pleasure; it was heard with adoration; and the beatified bridegroom promoted his sanctification, by covering the saint with his own cloak;

the

the company cried out, oh bleffedneſs! oh felicity! and the Moor received the compliments of all prefent upon his preferment to this holy dignity. However, I am told the faints are not all fo lucky as to acquire thefe extenfive privileges.

When a faint dies, they erect over his grave one of thofe little pavilions mentioned above. I had the good fortune to fee and fpeak with one of thefe reputed faints, and perhaps I may be thought to overcharge the picture, but I really do not. The particular whim of this man was to imitate with his lips the explofion of bombs and cannon. He went bellowing about the ſtreets all day long, and muttering like the ancient fybils. As he entered the room where we were, he began to breathe his divine effluvia all over it, going into every corner to let off his bombs and great guns with his mouth; he then partook
of

VOYAGE TO CADIZ. 201

of some fruits and other eatables which we gave him, and I was assured it would have been no hard matter to have prevailed upon the saint to drink wine, but for the many foreigners, and still more for the other Moors, who were present; although it is a capital crime in a Mahometan to taste wine: but in all countries it is enough that a man thinks he has some connection with the deity, to allow himself many privileges.

The wind that blew hard at sea, and kept us prisoners in Sallee for several days, abated at last, and suffered us to cross the bar safely. We eagerly seized this moment, and once more got to our ship, fully resolved not to hazard such another delay. We were desirous of going immediately to Cadiz: the length of our first voyage had greatly lowered our provisions, so that we had no time to lose.

We

We therefore got ready on the 10th of September, after lying at anchor fourteen days before Sallee. In vain did they endeavour to detain us; they made a signal from land the day before we set off; we sent directly to enquire what was the meaning of this signal, but there was no getting ashore; the bar was then unpassable, so we could get no information⁴⁷. The next day, the wind being favorable, we thought it best not to miss the opportunity, so we sailed for Cadiz, where we arrived in four days, on the 13th of September, at seven in the evening.

As we had touched upon the coast of Africa, we were of course to perform qua-

[47] During our stay at Cadiz, we received a letter from Sallee, by which we learnt, that the meaning of this signal was, they wanted us to come ashore, to receive a considerable present of provisions and refreshments, which the King of Morocco had ordered to be offered to us, upon his being informed of our arrival at Sallee.

rantine;

rantine; however, the physicians of health came and examined us, and as they found no sick on board, we were allowed to come ashore the very next day after our arrival. I waited on the Governor, to ask his consent, before I entered upon my operations; and then proceeded to the Marquis de la Victoria's to get leave to make my observations at the marine observatory, which was granted. Mr. Puyabry, the French consul, was so obliging as to take upon him all the necessary formalities for entering my instruments and the clocks into the city; this was no easy matter. All the permissions obtained for that purpose could not exempt us from a strict search at the custom house, and it was not till after many removals and much trouble, that my instruments were conveyed to the observatory. The clocks did not suffer the least injury from all this shaking: indeed Mr. Le Roy bent his whole attention

tion that way; but it may safely be affirmed, from the trial they have undergone in this voyage, that these clocks are very easily carried about, and that, with a little attention, they are not liable to stop or be discomposed, which is more perhaps than can be said of many others. I was soon informed that so far from being offended at the search my instruments had undergone, I might think myself well off if I were not searched at least as strictly, every time I went in or out at the city gates*. This custom appears the more ridiculous

---

* This search is made in the most ridiculous and indecent manner imaginable; no part of the clothing is exempt: their aim is to prevent the exportation of piastres, and consequently no one is suffered to go in or out of the town with more than five piastres about him, nor even with any considerable sum of French money. Tobacco is likewise prohibited; not long ago, this absurdity was carried so far, as even to throw away what

ridiculous to strangers, as it exists no where but at Cadiz.

The city of Cadiz is too well known to need a minute description; besides, there are but few monuments to excite admiration. The only remarkable edifice, or rather that will be so in time, if ever it is finished, is a church all built with marble. In fifty years, they have raised it to the height of thirty feet. The fortifications on the side of the land gate are very fine. The only walk about Cadiz is by the sea side, towards the road; it is called the *Lameda*; it is exposed to the scorching sun in the day time, and at night to the cold air of the sea, and to the least wind

what snuff you had in your snuff-box, and only leave enough for the day. The friars alone are exempted from the search; no doubt they are supposed to be incapable of making an ill use of the respect shewn to, and the confidence reposed in them.

that

that blows. This disagreeable situation prevents any trees from growing there above fifteen feet high. The prospect of the road, and the ships continually going in and out, is in my mind the only pleasure of the Lameda; however, as it is the only walk about town, the most brilliant company meets there every evening. Long cloaks and flapped hats must not appear there till the hour of the *Angelus*, but from that moment you do as you please. The foot walk is railed in on both sides with stone, and on the outside the coaches drive gently round, drawn by the prettiest mules in the world.

I might have saved myself the trouble of removing my instruments to Cadiz; I found a great many, and of the best construction, in the marine observatory. This observatory was erected under the direction of Mr. Godin. It is advantageously situated

situated by the sea-side, on the top of a
very high tower. The instruments are all
placed in a very spacious square saloon,
with windows on all sides, that command
the whole compass of the horizon; this
saloon opens into a gallery towards the
sea, whence you have a full view of the
whole sky, and still better than from the
platform of the saloon. The death of the
last director had occasioned some neglect
in the observatory, so that when I came
there, the apparatus was not quite in order; but Mr. Tofino, a lieutenant in the
service, who had been just appointed to succeed him, was preparing to restore and
put it to rights, and to enter upon a course
of observations, which will be the more
useful, as very few good ones have been
hitherto made in this city. I had been directed to enquire what observations had
been made relative to the determination
of the longitude of Cadiz, concerning
which

which there are great doubts; I made all the enquiries I possibly could, but was not able to find in the observatory, either observations, or the least sign of there having been any made, or any journal kept of such observations. The eclipse of 1764 was the only thing that appeared to have been accurately observed. I had it in charge to collect these observations, and Mr. Tofino obliged me with them. I found at Cadiz, Messieurs Doz and Medina, two lieutenants and astronomers, appointed by the Court of Spain to go to California, there to observe the transit of Venus, jointly with Mr. Chappe [*]. They were in hourly expectation of sailing, but the fleet being retarded, I had the satisfaction, during the whole time I staid at Cadiz, of having those gentlemen closely attend my observations; they were even so kind as to make some with me relative to my object.

A stay

[*] See page 8.

A stay of twenty days at Cadiz, enabled me to go through all the operations relative to my purpose, and I thought I might flatter myself with having thoroughly verified the time keepers in this place; it may well be supposed I was eager to draw up the results. The different aspects in which they may be viewed, would require long and minute discussions: I shall therefore confine myself to give the substance of them, sufficient to convey an idea of the success of the trial.

The result of the first observations I made at Cadiz was this:

That a ship which should have been at sea an hundred and nine days, would have been misled by one of these watches, only 56 minutes of a degree at her landing at Cadiz, which makes an error of about

fourteen

fourteen leagues in longitude [49]. By the other watch, which is that which had been opened at the island of Saint Pierre, the error would have been of 1 degree 45 minutes, that is, about twenty-seven leagues.

Now, the most experienced and skilful navigators make no scruple to own that in a run of two months, and sometimes less, they are apt to mistake by fifty or sixty leagues. How advantageous would it be then to the navy, to have a watch that, at the end of four months, would bring the longitude right, within fourteen leagues.

[49] In this determination, I suppose the longitude of Cadiz to be 8 deg. 21 min. but there is reason to think this city lies 12 minutes farther west than it has been placed hitherto, which lessens the error of the time keepers by just so many. They both agreed in placing Cadiz more westward than it stands in the maps.

Doubtless

Doubtless the success of this time keeper would have been perfectly satisfactory, had it not undergone a greater alteration than I could have wished, during my stay at Cadiz. The series of observations I made at that place, affords an instance of the compensations of irregularity that may happen in the movement of a watch, and shew the necessity of intermediate verifications, to judge of its march with any certainty in long voyages.

Having taken a sufficient number of observations, I sent my watches and instruments on board, and only waited for a fair wind to set sail, but was detained twelve days longer. This delay, the scantiness of our provisions, and the advanced season of the year, determined us to give up going to Lisbon, and it was resolved that we should go directly to Brest.

We sailed out of the road of Cadiz, on the 14th of October; an easterly wind drove us out to sea, and the next day we passed Cape St. Vincent. We then begun to steer our course northward; but the winds presently failed us, and we had almost a constant calm for a whole week, which was the more disagreeable, as we had a high and rolling sea. We imputed this swell, which even a calm could not abate, to some gust of wind that had lately blown in this latitude; this was the more probable, as we had observed the water very rough in the road, one day while we were yet at Cadiz, and it seemed to be very foul weather at sea. This reconciled us to the disappointment of having been wind bound.

It was about the latitude of Lisbon that we were becalmed; happily for us, what little wind there was, brought us on in our way, but this was so trifling, that it would have

have taken up a long time to have doubled Cape Finisterre. At last a favorable wind sprung up, and in a few days we got clear of the Spanish coast, and in the latitude of Brest.

We were going to reconnoitre the place on the 28th of October, and were preparing to go in, when a sudden gale from the south obliged us to give up our intention of landing, and to think of nothing but keeping in the latitude. The wind shifting more to the west, without abating in the least, the sea grew very tempestuous, and the horizon very thick. We were tossed for three days with a violent storm, waiting for the clearing up of the weather, and for a more tractable wind, to go and examine the land, which our estimate brought us nearer to than we wished. Our ship sustained several smart shocks, yet we were able to keep up our sails almost the whole time.

The

ARRIVAL AT BREST

The 30th of October in the morning the wind abated a little, and turned to north west; the horizon cleared up; all, in short, put on a promising aspect for our running towards the shore. At noon we discovered the isle of Ushant; leaving this island to the northward, we entered the passage of Iroise, which brought us fairly into the road of Brest, where we came to an anchor at seven in the evening.

Thus ended a voyage of four months and a half, lucky in every particular, I dare not add, successful in the execution; that must be left to the judgment of the public. Being landed at Brest, I made use of the first moments of fair weather, as they could not be expected to be frequent at this advanced season. I soon got a sufficient number of observations to close the trial of the time keepers. I then delivered them up into the hands of Mr. Le

Le Roy, and returned to Paris, where I arrived on the 28th of November. I had collected on board the ship all the obfervations I had made for trying the watches, fo that I was very foon able to give an account to the Academy both of my operations and of their refults.

FINIS.

www.ingramcontent.com/pod-product-compliance
Lightning Source LLC
Chambersburg PA
CBHW031832230426
43669CB00009B/1322